Decide to Lead

Decide to Lead

Building Capacity and Leveraging Change through Decision-Making

Mary B. Herrmann

ROWMAN & LITTLEFIELD
Lanham • Boulder • New York • London

Published by Rowman & Littlefield
A wholly owned subsidiary of The Rowman & Littlefield Publishing Group, Inc.
4501 Forbes Boulevard, Suite 200, Lanham, Maryland 20706
www.rowman.com

Unit A, Whitacre Mews, 26-34 Stannary Street, London SE11 4AB

British Library Cataloguing in Publication Information Available

Library of Congress Cataloging-in-Publication Data is Available

ISBN 978-1-4758-1304-3 (cloth: alk. paper)
ISBN 978-1-4758-1305-0 (pbk: alk. paper)
ISBN 978-1-4758-1306-7 (electronic)

∞™ The paper used in this publication meets the minimum requirements of American National Standard for Information Sciences Permanence of Paper for Printed Library Materials, ANSI/NISO Z39.48-1992.

Printed in the United States of America

Contents

Acknowledgments

I feel truly privileged and grateful to have been given the opportunity to dedicate my professional life to the service of students, families, and communities. As with most educational leaders, I assumed my positions with great humility and the deeply profound belief that I could make a positive difference. It has been quite a journey! I appreciate the inspiring school communities and valued colleagues along the way who have helped shape my learning, leadership, and decision-making.

I am thankful to my loving parents, Leo and Pauline Goebel, and sisters, Susan Goebel and Patricia Ziwisky, who from the beginning have helped me to value and appreciate the power of strong, caring relationships and service to others.

I am also profoundly grateful to my wonderful family, Scott Herrmann, Jessica Herrmann, Zachary Herrmann, and Michael Holden (all educators) who have unconditionally supported, inspired, and stretched me in countless ways. Thank you!

Introduction

Nothing is more difficult and therefore more precious than to be able to decide.
—Napoleon Bonaparte

TO DECIDE IS TO LEAD

A superintendent colleague shared a story about a conversation he had with his father-in-law, a retired career officer in the military. In discussing his new superintendent position, the father-in-law said, "You must make a lot of important decisions for all the money they are paying you." My colleague replied, "No, actually I don't personally make a lot of decisions, I have a great team of people who I trust and they make a lot of the decisions." His father-in-law was shocked—how could this be? The lively discussion that followed grappled with different perspectives around the nature, expectations, and role of the leader as decision-maker.

Despite style preferences in how decisions should be made, my colleague and his father-in-law emphatically agreed that decision-making is central to the leadership role. Decision-making is, and has always been, at the heart and soul of executive leadership activity.

Leaders are responsible and held accountable for the decisions that are made within the organization, whether they personally make them or not. It is this willingness to decide, with all its potential implications, that distinguishes leaders from others. So in essence, *to decide is to lead.*

This book will explore decision-making and all its complexity. Decision-making is defined *as the thoughtful and intentional choice of a particular course of action over another.* Decision-making, therefore, requires trade-offs, which often means letting go of something familiar to start something new. This opportunity to decide is incredibly empowering and when used responsibly and strategically can be a significant source of *leverage* for leading change in educational organizations.

The following assumptions related to decision-making are integral to the content of the book:

- *To decide to lead* is a courageous decision.
- There are many forces that shape decision-making.
- Leaders have the responsibility to model and insist on ethical and socially just decision-making.
- Leaders are responsible and held accountable for the decisions that are made whether they make them or not.
- The individual decision-making practices of the leader have an inevitable impact on the behaviors of others and how the organization as an entity goes about the processes of identifying problems, conceptualizing them, and finding ways of dealing with them.
- Leaders design and shape the conditions/architecture for decision-making in their organizations.
- An intentional focus on *decision-making as the work itself* can lead to improvements in the quality of decisions made throughout the organization.

The book, organized in three sections, examines decision-making through the lens of a leader. The first section explores what leaders *know*—knowledge of self, knowledge of others, and knowledge of one's community and context. Section II addresses how leaders *think*, with a focus on cognitive systems, the forces that influence decision-making, and conceptual frames that help leaders construct meaning. The third section examines what leaders *do* to set up the conditions for effective decision-making in their organizations. This section is focused on leader actions including building capacity, designing a decision-friendly organizational architecture, and employing and assessing decision-making models and processes.

Using the following conceptual model, the book addresses the question—*How do leaders understand, think about, and design the conditions for effective decision-making?*

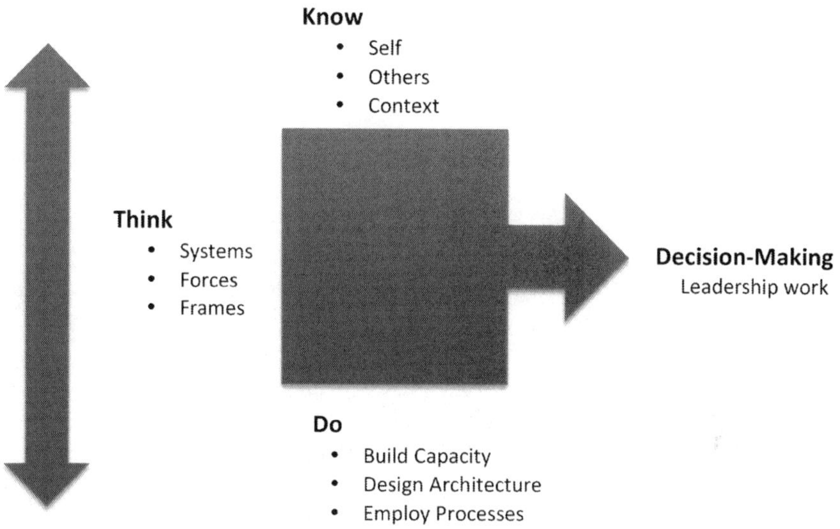
Know
Self
Others
Context
Think
Systems
Forces
Frames
Decision-Making
Leadership work
Do
Build Capacity
Design Architecture
Employ Processes

I

Know

Effective decision-making requires that we *know* and understand ourselves, others, and our community and context. In chapter 1 we examine who we are as leaders. We build on the assumption that the first courageous decision a leader makes is *to decide to lead.* We discuss why courage is essential by focusing on the emotional and personal investments leaders make and how their perceptions of the world shape the ways in which they lead. We also explore authenticity and how one's identity as a leader if too rigidly defined, can stifle personal growth.

Knowing self is essential to effective decision-making practices. How leaders think about and embrace their role as decision-maker, defines the nature and practice of decision-making activity within their organizations. *Leaders shape and define how the organization grapples with, frames, and responds to problems.*

Knowing *others* is also essential. In chapter 2 we examine how personal style coupled with personal beliefs about motivation, engagement, and social justice influence the way leaders shape the work environment for decision-making in their organizations.

The assumptions and beliefs leaders hold about what motivates people to act directly impact how they personally make decisions and more broadly empower others in decision-making processes. How leaders build trust, form relationships, and shape the organizational culture have significant implications for the quality of decisions that are made throughout the organization.

Knowing our *communities and context* is also critical. In chapter 3 we emphasize the importance of constantly striving to understand our community and ever-changing context. This chapter raises more questions than answers in tackling issues related to public value and the purpose of schooling. How leaders grapple with, construct meaning about, and communicate these greater purpose and contextual issues provides a frame for understanding and shaping their decision-making.

As we deliberate over our sense of purpose and our personal knowledge and understanding of the context in which we lead—we strive to better assess the extent and ways in which leaders *reflect their communities or strive to change them.*

Chapter One

In Search of Self

The self is not something ready-made, but something in continuous formation through choice of action. —John Dewey

DECIDING TO LEAD IS A COURAGEOUS CHOICE

The responsibilities associated with educational leadership positions are truly daunting. Feeling personally and professionally accountable for the community's children is an incredible responsibility and one that is never taken lightly. Whether caring for basic safety and security needs or ensuring that all students learn and grow, the responsibilities and decisions are tremendous in scope and significance.

Within this challenging context, *deciding to lead* is the leader's first courageous choice. When one identifies as a *leader* one becomes personally and emotionally invested in all the successes and failures associated with being held accountable for decisions. Assuming the role of leader is significant on both a personal and organizational level. Once a person assumes the role of decision-maker he is forever changed.

How leaders think about and embrace their role as decision-maker, defines the nature and practice of decision-making activity within their organizations. *Leaders shape and define how the organization grapples with, frames, and responds to problems*. Therefore it is appropriate that we begin the exploration of decision-making for leaders with a journey in *search of self*.

LEADERSHIP IS EMOTIONAL

We begin with the following assumption: *Leadership is emotional.* This is true for all levels of leadership and can be most appreciated when personally experienced. Those who have sat as the superintendent or CEO at the board table can relate to the unique feeling of being the *outsider* and *insider* concurrently. District leaders in particular, often exist in the gray areas of educational organizations. They are working between the lines, not a part of the governing board to which they report and not fully a part of the administrative team they lead. Whereas there are many members of the board and typically many other administrators, there is only one leader who is held accountable for all that happens (or doesn't happen) within the district.

The leader seated at the board table understands that leading an organization is more than playing a role—it is core to one's identity and perception of self. Everyday the leader brings to the position his hopes, fears, competencies, and vulnerabilities. Doing so makes the leadership experience a persistent struggle between *fulfilling one's deep sense of purpose and safely preserving one's sense of identity.*

The impact of one's emotional self is pervasive in all leadership activity. For this reason it is critical that when making decisions leaders understand how they *comprehend, understand*, and *regulate* their emotions. Since leadership is ultimately about influence, it is also important that leaders strive to better understand how their emotional selves are perceived and received by others.

Researchers have consistently found that emotional intelligence is essential to leadership effectiveness. Daniel Goleman, highly regarded for his expertise in this area, identifies and describes the following five components of emotional intelligence:

- *Self-awareness*—The ability to recognize and understand personal moods and emotions and drives, as well as their effect on others.
- *Self-regulation*—The ability to control or redirect disruptive impulses and moods, and the propensity to suspend judgment and to think before acting.
- *Internal motivation*—A passion to work for internal reasons, a joy in doing something, curiosity in learning, and a propensity to pursue goals with energy and persistence.
- *Empathy*—The ability to understand the emotional makeup of other people and treat people according to their emotional reactions.
- *Social skills*—Proficiency in managing relationships, finding common ground, and building rapport and networks.[1]

Researchers agree that leaders must consistently demonstrate fluency in both *comprehending* and *executing* each of these components of emotional intelligence to lead effectively.

When considering these components, making the distinction between *comprehension* and *execution* is critical. A leader may be able to comprehend what is going on appropriately, but struggle with how to execute or respond. For example, it is common for educational leaders to occasionally (sometimes frequently) feel like they are under attack. Whether at the board table, in a heated community forum, parent meeting, faculty meeting, or collective bargaining session, it is difficult for leaders to not *take it personally* when someone lashes out at them.

The leader may be able to accurately assess and understand why he feels a certain way, but still find it difficult to craft *an appropriate response.* It is not easy. It takes patience and practice for leaders to develop the discipline to accurately identify their emotions and consistently respond productively.

Even when a leader consistently demonstrates a high degree of emotional intelligence however, his/her emotions can still impact decision-making in significant ways. Dan Ariely, in his book *Predictably Irrational,*[2] cites research that suggests people who are in a highly emotional "aroused" state will make profoundly different choices then when they are in a neutrally emotional state. As a result, he emphasizes that it is important for leaders to acknowledge and accept that they are never fully "integrated" as human beings. Instead leaders must be able to recognize and be prepared to adjust in their role as decision-makers, both the Jekyll and Hyde aspects of themselves.

Being prepared and personally adjusting is required in all aspects of one's work as a leader. For example, since leaders are constantly negotiating with others they need to be mindful of the *emotional dimensions* at the heart of any negotiating situation. Fisher and Shapiro in their book, *Beyond Reason: Using Emotions as You Negotiate,*[3] identify five core concerns that are important to almost everyone in virtually every negotiation. The core concerns include: *appreciation*, *affiliation*, *autonomy*, *status*, and *role.* Leaders should always be prepared to positively address these core concerns both personally and in their response to others. When leaders address these emotional concerns in their interactions with others they enhance the likelihood that negotiating and shared decision-making practices will *feel* more emotionally satisfying to those involved and will ultimately result in better outcomes.

REACTIVE TENDENCIES AND CREATIVE COMPETENCIES

In addition to understanding and regulating our emotional selves, Bob Anderson, one of the authors of the *Leadership Circle Profile,*[4] asserts that how leaders perceive their world matters significantly in their leadership roles. In describing one dimension of his comprehensive framework, he argues that when leaders unwittingly perceive their world as a fearful place they are more likely to respond with "reactive tendencies" rather than "creative competencies."

Anderson describes *creative competencies* as those researched "best practice" competencies that foster leading with vision, bringing out the best in others, enhancing one's own development, acting with integrity and courage, and improving organizational systems. *Reactive tendencies*, on the other hand, are leadership styles that emphasize caution over creating results, self-protection over productive engagement, and aggression over building alignment. Reactive tendencies overemphasize the focus on gaining approval from others, protecting oneself, and getting results through high control tactics.

This is critical insight for leaders. Leaders need to know that how they personally perceive the world directly impacts how they shape and define decision-making within their organizations. If leaders unwittingly experience the world as a fearful place, where "others are out to get us," they are more likely to engage more reactively, *with behaviors like excessive control, aloofness, criticalness, and approval seeking.* When the leader engages in these types of excessive behaviors, there are significant implications for all decision-making within the organization.

For example, when a leader tends to engage in *excessive control behaviors* it is often driven by personal fears of feeling inadequate and never quite measuring up. These *excessive control* behaviors are not conducive to building trust and empowering others. When leaders use excessive control all organizational decision-making is filtered through a fear-based, narrow, rigid, and highly controlled lens.

Other *reactive* strategies like *aloofness and criticalness* help leaders feel competent, more intelligent, and superior. To accomplish this sense of being "at the top of the organization," the leader behaves in ways that diminish the contributions of others. It makes sense that if the leader maintains a comfortable distance from the real work and culture of the organization he/she can be more critical of it. Organizational decision-making under these reactive leadership conditions may appear to be more *hands off–hands on*. In other words, the leader may not engage in the act of making a decision, but be critical of the decision (and decision-makers) after it is made.

Excessive *approval seeking* holds the inner assumption that one's true value and worth lies in the hands of others. Leaders are reticent to do anything that may cause their approval ratings to diminish. Driven by the need to survive, conflict is avoided at all costs, even if it means compromising one's own integrity and beliefs. The leader's decision-making (and ultimately the organization's) consistently reflects what he perceives to be the "safest choices."

If instead, leaders perceive the world not as a place to fear but rather as a place of great opportunity, they are better equipped to engage in more *creative competencies* such as leading with vision, acting with integrity, and bringing out the best in others. Decision-making under these conditions is grounded in trust and transparency, and involves consistently engaging and empowering others in a wide array of creative ways.

Becoming a better leader by increasing one's knowledge of self is challenging work. Soliciting meaningful input from others can help leaders get to know themselves in new and different ways. Three-sixty assessments (like the one embedded in the Leadership Circle profile) and other measures, when administered in a trusting environment, can help leaders better understand how they impact others. When leaders seek to better understand all aspects of themselves they become better equipped to adjust and adapt their behaviors to become more effective. But that does not suggest that changing habits of mind and practice are easy. The reality is, rethinking one's personal identity, or "authentic self," is far more complicated.

AUTHENTICITY AND LEARNING

Earlier in our discussion we alluded to the constant tension between *fulfilling one's sense of efficacy* or purpose as a leader and *preserving one's identity*. Leaders have long believed that the best way to be true to oneself or one's identity is to be *authentic*. When leaders behave authentically, when their actions are consistent with their perceptions of themselves, they feel grounded and comfortable. They act in ways that feel genuine and true to self. According to Herminia Ibarra in the article "The Authenticity Paradox,"[5] however, authenticity in leadership can also be limiting. She states, "the notion of adhering to one 'true self' flies in the face of much research on how people evolve with experience."

To evolve, leaders need to continually embrace opportunities for learning new behaviors rather than retreat into the comfort of authentic practice. Ibarra argues, "the only way to avoid being pigeonholed and ultimately become better leaders is to do the things that a rigidly authentic sense of self would keep us from doing."[6]

As educational leaders, it is easy to become authentically "pigeonholed." The people with whom leaders work and serve in their schools and communities expect them to be confident about what they believe and competent in their ability to lead. A clear and firm sense of self exudes confidence and helps leaders navigate choices and progress toward their goals. But in increasingly complex conditions, if one's sense of self is too rigid, it can also become an anchor that impedes one's ability to make the decisions that will move the organization forward.

In essence, our sense of self is reflected in and shaped to a large extent by our "mindsets." According to Carol Dweck, "the view you adopt for yourself profoundly affects the way you lead your life."[7] She makes the distinction between a *fixed and growth mindset.* The *fixed mindset* is based on the belief that one's qualities (intelligence, moral character, etc.) are "set in stone." The *growth mindset*, on the other hand, is based on the belief that you can *cultivate your basic qualities through your efforts.*

In the TED talk, "Why You Think You're Right Even When You're Wrong,"[8] Julie Galef suggests that related to the more cognitively based, *fixed and growth mindsets* popularized by Dweck, there are distinct *emotional mindsets* that represent profoundly different perspectives and greatly impact judgment and decision-making. Galef begins with the question: *What do you most yearn for? Do you yearn to defend your own beliefs or do you yearn to see the world as clearly as you possibly can?* She said people respond to that question in ways that are consistent with an *emotional mindset* being either what she refers to as *a soldier, prone to defending your viewpoint at all costs—or a scout, spurred by curiosity.*

Educational leaders, to meet the demands of an increasingly complex environment, must continually look outside themselves to gain new perspectives and discover novel behaviors and approaches to decision-making and problem-solving even if doing so initially feels uncomfortable. In other words, it is essential for leaders to be open to adaptation and new ways of behaving, to think flexibly about who they are, and to embrace *growth* and *scout* mindsets that encourage learning through active trial and error.

GROWING OUR JUDGMENT, MENTAL CAPACITY, AND RESILIENCY

In our *search for self,* we grow to understand our emotional self and how it impacts our leadership. We learn that how we perceive our world drives our tendencies to be reactive or builds our competencies to be creative. We also recognize that our authentic self is not a static condition, but a constantly adapting "work in progress."

As "works in progress" it is also important to explore our perceptions of ourselves in relation to our own mental models and frames of reference. To do so we need to develop the capacity to see and understand ourselves, and our organizations at a higher level of mental complexity.

In other words, to become more effective decision-makers, leaders must become more sophisticated thinkers who are skilled at reframing, adding new frames and stretching and developing their minds to address deeper levels of complexity.

Leaders must also understand that how they frame and think about a situation (particularly a difficult one) impacts how they respond. When leaders can embrace a playful, growth-oriented mindset that fosters constant learning through trial and error they also build the resiliency that is truly essential for survival and effectiveness. For most leaders, it is not about whether you get knocked down (because you most certainly will) it is about getting back up, learning from the experience, and growing stronger. As Maya Angelou so eloquently stated,[9] "we may encounter many defeats, but we must not be defeated. It may even be necessary to encounter the defeat so that we can know who we are."

ETHICS, CHARACTER, AND LEGACY

The leader's sense of self and self-efficacy also evolves with experience. In the book *Life Cycles of Leadership*,[10] Uebbing and Ford describe one's role as a leader as continually transforming through different stages. Personal awareness of one's perceptions of these stages is important for the leader. The stages include *survival*, *creativity*, and *legacy*. For the most part leaders mature through the life cycle and ultimately spend less time on survival and more on creation and legacy. However, "a leader can deal with all three contexts on any given day. And a leader who has entered the legacy phase can easily return to the survival stage in the blink of an eye."[11]

In all phases or stages of one's journey as a leader, however, one's strong, ethical character must remain constant. In his book *The Road to Character*,[12] David Brooks discusses the difference between the *résumé* virtues and the *eulogy* virtues. He describes the résumé virtues as "the ones you list on your résumé, the skills that you bring to the job market and that contribute to external success. The eulogy virtues are deeper. They're the virtues that get talked about at your funeral, the ones that exist at the core of your being—whether you are kind, brave, honest or faithful; what kind of relationships you formed."

In our *search of self*, the virtues espoused in one's eulogy are the ones that will have the greatest, long-term impact on one's effectiveness as a leader.

Questions for Further Reflection

1. In what ways are you "vulnerable" as a leader?
2. In considering your personal emotional intelligence—what are your greatest strengths? Areas in need of growth?

3. How do you perceive the world? Are you driven more by "reactive tendencies" or "creative competencies"?
4. To what extent and in what ways have you adapted your authentic self? How do you continue to grow and stretch yourself?
5. How would you describe your *eulogy virtues*? How would others describe them?

Chapter Two

Motivation, Trust, and Engagement

> True leaders understand that leadership is not about them but about those they serve. It is not about exalting themselves but about lifting others up. —Sheri L. Dew

Effective decision-making requires *knowledge of others*. In chapter 1 we focused on understanding self and how our perceptions of self shape our actions as leaders. This chapter examines how personal style coupled with personal beliefs about motivation, engagement, and social justice influence the way leaders shape the work environment for decision-making in their organizations.

The assumptions and beliefs leaders hold about what motivates people to act directly impact how they personally make decisions and, more broadly, empower others in decision-making processes. There has been extensive research across a wide array of disciplines related to motivation and employee engagement.

BEYOND THEORY X AND THEORY Y

It is important to begin our discussion with a little background in management theory by reviewing the highlights of Douglas McGregor's work related to Theory X and Theory Y.[1] In essence, *Theory X* and *Theory Y* represent two sets of assumptions about human nature and human behavior that are relevant to the work of leaders. *Theory X represents a negative view of human nature* that assumes individuals generally dislike work, are irresponsible, and require close supervision to do their jobs. *Theory Y denotes a positive view of human nature* and assumes individuals are generally industrious, creative, and able to assume responsibility and exercise self-control in their jobs.

This is significant because the assumptions that leaders hold about human nature shape their management practices—so a leader whose assumptions are more consistent with Theory X will manage very differently than one who makes Theory Y assumptions. These assumptions also significantly impact the overall decision-making architecture of the organization. For example, McGregor believed that Theory Y assumptions would lead to more effective management. He identified organization-wide approaches that included decentralization of decision-making authority, delegation, job enlargement, and participative management.

Since the time this work was first introduced in the 1950s, it has had a profound impact on the way people view, lead, and interact with organizations. Many researchers have enhanced, supported, or refuted McGregor's full body of assumptions and management principles, but few argue that in its simplest form the work has helped leaders draw the conceptual linkages between the assumptions they make about human nature and how they shape their management styles and practices.

MOTIVATION BEYOND CARROTS AND STICKS

Today leaders continue to grapple with some of these same assumptions, but are now able to draw on a stronger research base related to human behavior. This increased knowledge has helped inform leadership and decision-making practices in significant ways.

Daniel Pink, in his book *Drive*,[2] describes some of the highlights of what researchers have learned about motivation. In doing so he makes the case that it is necessary to more fully align our organizational practices with what we now know about human motivation and behavior. His work has significant implications for decision-making in our schools and school districts. According to Pink, people are not motivated by carrots and sticks, but instead by the opportunity to experience *autonomy*, *mastery*, and *purpose*.

School personnel, like other workers want purposeful work, want a say in what they do, and want the support of their administrators and colleagues to help them achieve mastery. Schools that focus on compliance to rules and highly prescriptive and routine practices are uninspiring to both students and staff. We will address this further in chapter 7 in our discussion of organizational structures that foster effective decision-making.

When leaders understand principles of motivation and are able to differentiate and employ them effectively they demonstrate that they are invested in their people. Leaders further demonstrate their commitment to the greater organizational mission when they hire, develop, and retain excellent personnel. Of the factors that schools can control, we know that effective teachers can have the greatest impact on student learning and growth. High-quality decision-making that ensures a focus on hiring, developing, and retaining excellent people should be a top priority in schools.

Sydney Finkelstein in a *Harvard Business Review* article titled the "Secrets of Superbosses"[3] states that one thing that distinguishes the super successful leader from others is the ability to recognize, recruit, and retain exceptionally talented individuals. In reality, this doesn't always happen. In schools, like other organizations, it is easy to *sometimes settle* in our hiring practices, by not always choosing the most creative, competent, or intelligent person. This happens for many reasons. The candidate may not *fit* with the rest of the team, or match the culture of the school or district, or be the top choice of board members or other teachers or administrators. Sometimes leaders *settle* in hiring decisions because there are other good options and it may feel like a battle not worth fighting. In considering the big picture, however, personnel selections are high-leverage/high-impact decisions and as politically charged as they may be, leaders need to ensure that the very best people are hired to serve the community's children.

The reality is, sometimes finding great people is easier than keeping them. Retaining great people requires a longer and more sustained and systemic effort from leaders. Leaders need to be highly intentional and focused on building a strong culture, characterized by a positive climate. *So what does that look like?* According to research,[4] school cultures that contribute to improved student learning have the following:

- A strong *professional community* where all adults are meaningfully connected to grow and change. Their expertise is valued in decision-making and they share a collective responsibility for all students learning.
- A way of integrating and constructing new knowledge and innovation through *organizational learning.*
- *Trust*—the result of several dispositions working together—integrity, concern for others, competence, and reliability.

Ultimately, leaders recognize that nothing is more significant in shaping a positive, socially just climate and culture than a strong foundation of trust. As Colin Powell so eloquently stated,[5] "Leadership ultimately comes down to creating conditions of trust within an organization. Good leaders are ones who are trusted by followers."

Leaders must be cognizant of how their routine behaviors and decisions impact trust, relationships, and perceptions of social justice within the school or district. In the book, *The Trust Factor: Strategies for School Leaders,*[6] Combs and colleagues distinguish between behaviors that are *trust builders* from those that are *trust busters*. If leaders are not self-aware and intentional about their words and actions, it is easy to engage in behaviors that "bust" trust. These behaviors include such things as a lack of follow-through, ignoring incompetence, gossiping, failing to regulate their emotions, playing favorites, and behaving in culturally incompetent or socially unjust ways. On the other hand, leaders can *build* trust by consistently engaging in trustworthy behaviors that demonstrate competence, care, character, and effective, transparent communication. Some specific examples of how leaders build trust include:

- Being present, visible, and actively listening.
- Being kind, empathic, and respectful of people and their time.
- Being transparent and communicating effectively.
- Maintaining confidentiality.
- Setting high expectations for self and others, and providing the resources and support to meet them.
- Using power wisely, empowering others, and delegating strategically.
- Learning from mistakes and blaming processes—not people.

To be effective, leaders must be both personally trustworthy and trusting of others.

ENGAGEMENT

The benefits of a strong foundation of trust are far reaching and can lead to higher levels of engagement. This is particularly important because focused *engagement* is key to productive behavior. High levels of engagement are also essential in building organizational capacity. From a holistic perspective, work performance, and decision-making improve when the feelings, attitudes, and behaviors of people are positively aligned. For example, *employee satisfaction (a feeling), is reflected in a sense of commitment (attitude) and is demonstrated through engagement (behavior).*[7]

Engagement is defined as the state of emotional and intellectual involvement and commitment that leads people to do their best work. According to Barto,[8] "We see engagement when people: Say, Stay and Strive—Say: consistently speak positively about the organization to co-workers, potential employees and customers. Stay: Have an intense desire to be part of the organization, and Strive—Exert extra effort and engage in behaviors that contribute to organizational success."

To ensure high levels of engagement, it is essential for school leaders to understand what is motivational to their people and recognize that with this knowledge comes the responsibility to personalize and differentiate their practices. Leaders need to acknowledge that even though there are certain motivational principles that can inform leadership practices, *one size does not fit all.*

Questions for Further Reflection

1. What motivates me?
2. What do I believe motivates others?
3. What "trust building" behaviors do I exhibit? What "trust busting" behaviors?
4. What does engagement mean (look like, feel like) in my work setting?
5. What can I do as a leader to enhance engagement in my school or district?

Chapter Three

Community and Context

Education is the most powerful weapon you can use to change the world. —
Nelson Mandela

In chapter 1 we focused on understanding who we are and how our perception of self shapes our actions as leaders. In chapter 2 we sought to better assess our own beliefs about working with others. In chapter 3 we are shifting our focus from a search for self to the continuous journey of seeking to better understand our community and context. As we deliberate over our sense of purpose we strive to better assess the extent to which we, as leaders, *reflect our communities or strive to change them.*

This chapter raises more questions than answers in tackling issues related to public value and the purpose of schooling. How leaders grapple with and construct meaning around these greater purpose and contextual issues provides a frame for understanding and shaping their decision-making.

LEADING FOR PUBLIC VALUE

In their book, *Ports in a Storm: Public Management in a Turbulent World,*[1] John Donohue and Mark Moore assert that public organizations have the same challenges related to creating value as do organizations in the private sector. Most educational leaders would agree with the authors that in public organizations (such as schools), however, the context and process is far more complex. The authors indicate that when contemplating public value there are at least two critical areas of questioning. The first area focuses on *who are the clients or the citizens and taxpayers in whose name the governmental entity (or in our case the school/district) acts? And, how do those clients become articulate and clear about their views on which values and outcomes are worth pursuing?* The second area of questioning relates *to the dimensions of performance that those who are identified as the proper arbiters of public value embrace.*

These are highly complex and often politically charged questions for school leaders. Who are the *arbiters* in their communities? Are they the students, parents, teachers, taxpayers, government officials, business leaders, or all of these? And to what end? How do these *arbiters* understand and define the purpose of public education and what do they expect from their schools? How do they describe the indicators of success? Are they seeking improved performance on test scores, a reduction in costs, equity, capable citizens, socialization, or all of these things and more? To what extent are they interested in preserving the status quo? Are they committed to serving the greater good? The questions continue.

School leaders are constantly (and carefully) navigating the complex territory surrounding these questions in increasingly diverse and ever changing communities. The effort to understand these fundamental issues plays out differently depending on *what is being asked, who it benefits, and who is asking*. How leaders answer these fundamental questions can have significant implications in the way they lead and whether they choose (or have the opportunity) to stay in their community. In other words, how these questions are understood and acted upon contribute to the leaders' overall sense of satisfaction or longevity in their districts. Do these answers reflect a leadership match or a philosophical disconnect? To what extent are the answers to these questions consistent with one's own values, beliefs, sense of social justice, and commitment to service?

Constantly faced with growing needs and multiple (often disparate) agendas it is essential to routinely grapple with the question—*Who do we serve?* For example, *who do we serve* is at the forefront of leadership efforts when faced with the need for a referendum to increase educational funding or improve capital projects. Who is given voice and who will prove to be most influential? Who holds the power? Who is silenced? Given these questions, what leverage does an educational leader have and how does she employ that leverage?

Who do we serve is always at the heart of service in diverse communities—how do leaders give voice to those who have been left out or silenced, because of race, gender, sexual orientation, economic status, language, religious beliefs, and so on? How do leaders make decisions that advocate for the greater good, when the community's *arbiters* may not directly benefit?

WHY SCHOOL?

Moving from questions related to who has power and influence to questions of purpose or ends, adds further complexity to the leader's role within the educational context. This in part is a consequence of having little consensus around the purpose of schooling in the United States. Although the concept of a free, K–12 public education has historically been valued, there has been considerable debate and discourse around what public schools should and should not do, intentionally leaving ample (although recently less so) space for local communities and educational leaders to navigate through the messiness.

The debate around purpose is significant. As a case in point, Willona Sloan in an article references a TED.com conversation that addressed the question "In your opinion, what should be the purpose of education?" When the lively TED discussion was brought to a close, the facilitator noted that there were 365 recorded comments and 365 distinct articulations of what the purpose of education should be. He emphasized the significance of this by stating, "The process to develop a consensus on this is beyond the scope and purpose of this conversation. However, I do hope that it is understood that this question and its answer are the shapers of education systems and, in turn, cultures."[2]

Given that much of our sense of educational purpose has been shaped by forces outside our districts and void of local community conversations that challenge assumptions and grapple with complex ideas—*How do educational leaders talk about purpose and the things that matter?*

EDUCATIONAL DISCOURSE

The language leaders choose shapes their own leadership behavior and the behavior of others. Thomas Armstrong,[3] in his book, *The Best Schools*, refers to two distinctly different perspectives characterized by language and phrases that shape the way we think about schooling. He refers to these as different "educational discourses" or institutionalized ways of thinking and defining boundaries. He labels these broad perspectives as *the academic achievement discourse* and *the human development discourse.*

The *academic achievement discourse* is identified by language that describes *high levels of accountability* and supports the following assumptions:

- Academic content and skills are the most important things to be learned.
- Measurement of achievement occurs through grades and standardized testing.

- The academic curriculum is rigorous, uniform, and required for all students.
- Learning takes place as preparation for the future.

The *human development discourse*, on the other hand, is identified by an emphasis on the *evolving nature of human beings* rather than academic content and is based on the following assumptions:

- Becoming a whole human being is the most important aspect of learning.
- Evaluating growth is a meaningful, ongoing, and qualitative process.
- Curriculum is flexible, individualized, and gives students meaningful choices.
- Learning encompasses the past, present, and future of every student.

School leaders must be cognizant of the language that is used in their communities around the purposes of schooling. What can be learned from the casual conversations in coffee houses, neighborhood gatherings, and among parents on the soccer fields? What about the local business community and local alliances? Is there a commitment to all students in the community? Is there talk of social justice and issues of equity? Does the language used suggest a highly academic, achievement-oriented community or one that espouses a more holistic and human development perspective? Leaders can help define and clarify purpose by being intentional in their own language and action.

The leader's beliefs and language around purpose are integral to how and why decisions are made—In what ways does the leader's decision-making and problem-solving articulate a clear sense of purpose and shape the conditions to produce the kinds of human beings that the district aspires to develop? Through their language and decision-making *do leaders reflect or shape their communities*?

Questions for Further Reflection

1. What do you understand the purpose of schooling to be?
2. Who do you serve? Who are the *arbiters* in your community? Under what circumstances and to what ends?
3. Assess in your school community the language that is commonly used. Are the words used like accountability, alignment, failure, benchmarks, achievement, and performance? Or are they words like growth, character, developmentally appropriate, curiosity, and creativity?
4. What language do you use as a leader? Are you inclined to reflect your community or strive to change it?
5. In what ways do you lead for social justice?

II

Think

Effective decision-making requires that leaders are aware of how they and others process information. For this reason, section II focuses on *thinking* capabilities and limitations. We explore how leaders *think*, with a focus on cognitive systems; the forces that influence decision-making; and the conceptual frames that help leaders construct meaning.

Chapter 4 focuses specifically on *the forces that can shape our decisions*. The chapter provides a quick overview of two distinct modes of processing information, (*System 1 and System 2*) and a brief description of just a few of the many cognitive biases and filters that influence decision-making.

In chapter 5 the focus shifts from *forces that influence decisions* to *conceptual frames that assist leaders* in constructing meaning and making sense of their world. The chapter begins with a brief historical perspective of the primary schools of thought related to the *ways in which decision-making occurs* in organizations and provides some reflective tools to assist leaders in assessing their decision-making processes. The discussion that follows moves from a focus on the *way* in which decisions are made to *how* the leader thinks about, understands, and defines the context for decision-making. Some useful conceptual frames are shared.

Chapter Four

Forces That Shape Our Decisions

> We think, each of us, that we're much more rational than we are. And we think that we make our decisions because we have good reasons to make them. Even when it's the other way around—We believe in the reasons, because we've already made the decision. —Daniel Kahneman

We have thus far considered our perceptions of self, principles of motivation, and leading others, and the greater context of understanding and articulating purpose and value. As we will discuss in this chapter, effective decision-making also requires us to focus on our own *thinking* capabilities and limitations. This chapter will focus specifically on *the forces that can shape our decisions.*

Decision-making is complicated. Even when we feel we know ourselves and our organizations well and have a good understanding of how to interact with and influence others, there are still psychological, neurological, and other irrational forces that greatly impact what we think and do.

Over the past several decades, cognitive psychologists and behavioral decision researchers have made tremendous gains in their understanding of how human beings engage in processing information and making decisions. Many concur that there are (at least) two distinct modes of thinking processes. Daniel Kahneman,[1] winner of the Nobel prize in economics and author of the book *Thinking Fast and Slow*, labels these cognitive processing modes as *System 1* and *System 2*. According to Kahneman, *System 1 thinking is automatic, instinctive, and emotional.* It relies on mental shortcuts that generate intuitive answers to problems as they arise. *In contrast System 2 thinking is slow, logical, and deliberate.*

Each of the two modes of thinking has distinct advantages and disadvantages. In many cases, *System 1* takes in information and reaches correct conclusions efficiently and almost effortlessly by simply using intuition and rules of thumb. At other times, however, these *System 1* shortcuts cause problems and lead us astray in our decision-making. When this occurs it is only the slower more methodical *System 2* thinking that can inform us when our intuition is wrong or our emotions have clouded our judgment.

Since *System 2* thinking however, is slow and takes considerable time and effort, we frequently rely almost exclusively on *System 1* thinking. Unfortunately, this overreliance on *System 1* allows our intuitions or emotions to go unchecked by analysis and deliberation, which not surprisingly, often results in poor decisions. Kahneman suggests that to consistently make better decisions we need to "slow down and let System 2 take control."[2] This of course is a huge challenge given the incredible demand for fast-paced decision-making and problem-solving that has become routine for educational leaders. We will discuss this further in later chapters.

BIASES IN DECISION-MAKING

Extensive reliance on *System 1* processing also leads to biases in decision-making. It is important to recognize, however, that even when we are more deliberate we can be susceptible to biases. Therefore, it is essential that leaders are aware of and can challenge bias in decision-making both personally and organizationally. To that end, the next several paragraphs identify, describe, and stretch leaders to consider some common biases/traps in organizational decision-making (adapted from work summarized in Mind Tools).[3]

We begin with *confirmation bias.* This happens when you look for information that supports your existing beliefs, and reject data that go against what you believe. This can lead you to make biased decisions, because you don't factor in all of the relevant information. A recent study found that confirmation bias can affect the way that people view statistics, demonstrating that people have a tendency to infer information from statistics that supports their existing beliefs, even when the data support an opposing view. This is a particularly important insight for educational leaders who expect staff members to use a wide array of data to better inform instruction and guide school improvement efforts.

School leaders need to consider—*Have we provided the training and resources needed to help our teachers and administrators consider data from multiple perspectives and to use it intelligently and appropriately in their decision-making?*

Anchoring is the tendency to jump to conclusions and base your final judgment on information or perceptions gained early on in the decision-making process. Think of this as a "first impression" bias. Once you form an initial picture of a situation, it's hard to see other possibilities.

School leaders need to consider—*To what extent and in what ways, do we set the expectations and provide the time and "push back" needed for getting past "first impression" bias?*

The *recognition/status quo bias* entices individuals to seize upon the familiar rather than search for creative alternatives. The familiar is comfortable, so there is a natural tendency for people to accept without critical examination alternatives that support the status quo. Options that maintain the existing situation are favored over those that cause change because individuals don't want to rock the boat.

School leaders need to consider—*To what extent can we find compelling evidence for change and then connect the desired change or new initiative to something that is already familiar and comfortable?*

We succumb to the *overconfidence bias* when we place too much faith in our own knowledge and opinions. We may also believe that our contribution to a decision is more valuable than it actually is. We might combine this bias with anchoring, and act on hunches, because we have an unrealistic view of our own decision-making ability.

School leaders need to consider—*To what extent and in what ways do we model and encourage diverse and collaborative decision-making processes that routinely challenge assumptions and use a wide array of data?*

The *fundamental attribution error* is the tendency to blame others when things go wrong instead of looking objectively at the situation. In particular, you may blame or judge someone based on a stereotype or a perceived personality flaw.

School leaders need to consider—*To what extent do we reflect on our own behavior and learn from it? Do we look non-judgmentally at situations and the people involved in them? How often do we blame people rather than the process?*

The *anxiety driven bias* can also lead us astray. Researchers have found that high stakes decisions[4] —those that involve high levels of uncertainty—cause people to be more receptive to advice and less discriminating. When a person is feeling anxious these tendencies can combine in a way that can be harmful. Studies found that people who were made to feel anxious were more open to, and more likely to rely on, advice even when they knew that the person offering it had a conflict of interest and the advice was bad.

School leaders need to consider—*How can I take more control over the conditions under which I make decisions and when possible refrain from making major decisions until I am better positioned to be thoughtful and reflective?*

In addition to the sampling of biases stated above, there are other factors and filters that leaders should be aware of in their decision-making. In the article, "Fooled by Experience,"[5] the authors, Emre Soyer and Robin Hogarth provide further insight into how *experience* can influence decision-making. They contend "although experience seems like a reliable guide, sometimes it fools us rather than makes us wiser." This happens because we view the past through numerous filters that distort our perceptions.

The authors identify three types of filters that routinely distort how we see things; they include *a bias for outcomes*, our *circle of advisors*, and our own *limited reasoning abilities.* A bias for outcomes causes us to favor successes over the processes that lead to them, and can contribute to unethical behaviors that defend the "end" as justification for the means. It also undermines the potential of studying failure as a powerful tool for learning.

For school leaders, in a time of high quantitatively measurable accountability, we may be more likely to quickly discard "holistically" positive programs, over *teach to the test* practices, because they don't immediately demonstrate improved student performance on standardized tests. School leaders need to consider—*How many initiatives do we implement one year, only to move onto the next best thing the following year?*

Our closest advisors in an effort to be supportive can also distort our perceptions by sharing only those things that they think we want to hear and thereby censoring the information we receive. It is critical to have at least one loyal colleague who disagrees and constantly pushes us to consider all the implications and possibilities inherent in a decision. School leaders need to consider—*Is there someone on my team who plays this essential role?*

Lastly, just because we are "human," we are innately limited in our reasoning abilities. These limitations contribute to our personal inability to see the whole and eliminate biases resulting in our personal inclination to think that *we know more than we do and have more control over outcomes than we truly have.* What makes this particularly challenging for those serving in public leadership positions is that others *also* think that we have more control than we do. This further perpetuates the expectation that school or district leaders should be able to *fix everything.* School leaders need to consider—*How can I better recognize my own limitations and feel confident in being transparent with others?*

In addition to the biases and filters that can distort our thinking, our overreliance on *System 1* has another negative effect: It can lead to poor follow-through on our plans, despite our best intentions and genuine desire to achieve our goals. That's because *System 1* is simpler and easier—it tends to focus on concrete, immediate payoffs, distracting us from the abstract, long-term consequences of our decisions.

In a world where we can gain immediate access to others (and they to us) through tweets, text messages, emails, and so on, there is little patience for lengthy, more deliberate processes. Addressing everybody's concerns *immediately* becomes the expectation for public officials, even though thoughtful more deliberate processes of problem-solving that are aligned with long-term goals are likely to be more effective. For example, when a board member has a conversation with an angry parent at a soccer game, the source of anger for that parent may easily become the most pressing decision-making issue of the day for the school administrator. Ensuring the "quick fix" happens has become a survival strategy for many school leaders.

The following is another example of how the "quick fix" shapes our behavior in significant ways. Pressed with the need for a safe and secure environment in our schools we may immediately push for more visible security measures (i.e., safety personnel, cameras, visitor check-in procedures) and think we have solved our problem. Although these may strengthen our perception of safety they do not address some of the most significant underlying issues that may contribute to a lack of security. These underlying issues may include feelings of alienation or boredom, bullying, harassment, racism, and so on—factors that may be truly impacting student and staff well-being and one's sense of a safe environment. To address these issues requires leaders to slow down and deeply engage with others in a slower, messier, more deliberate, and sometimes (more politically) heated process.

There is also a wide array of examples of *System 1* biases in our human resource practices. We easily make assumptions about people based on where they live, where they went to school, other districts in which they worked, how much we may have in common with them, and how similar they may be to us. We initially respond in an emotionally favorable way to people who seem more like us. Acting on these biases has significant long-term implications in education where leaders need to build a more diverse teaching and administrative force.

According to Howard Ross,[6] the author of "3 Ways to Make Less Biased Decisions," a recent US Equal Employment Opportunity Commission report identified

> "Unconscious bias and perceptions about African Americans" as one of seven "major obstacles hindering equal opportunities for African Americans in the federal work force." In fact, simply having a name that sounds black can reduce the chance of you getting an interview, according to a study conducted by researchers at MIT and the University of Chicago. The research showed that this is true even at companies that are actively looking for diversity in hiring. Similar trends have been identified in virtually every aspect of the talent management system. For example, another study from the University of Warsaw, found that women described with feminine job titles (e.g. "chairwoman") are perceived (by men) to be as significantly less warm and marginally less competent than women with masculine job titles. And men reported that they were less likely to hire these women.

To address these biases school leaders need to be proactive and explicit in critically examining and better developing human resource personnel and practices within their districts.

Although there are many concerns associated with *System 1* thinking, there are also times when the intuitive and emotional reactions can serve as important inputs in the decision-making process. For example, as district leaders it is not uncommon to be contacted by search firms that suggest how perfectly compatible you may be for a position the firm is trying to fill. You are honored to be contacted and feel obligated to consider the opportunity. Sometimes it may be a good match and worth considering. It is essential to recognize however, that if the new opportunity triggers a strong emotional response, it is important to pay attention and carefully consider whether the move is worthwhile or too risky. The *System 1* emotional, *I feel it in my gut*, response should not be ignored, but also should not be the only factor considered. It should be weighed through thoughtful *System 2* deliberation against other factors that may be underappreciated by *System 1* such as the long-term strategic value of changing positions.

The reality is that engaging *System 2* requires exerting cognitive effort, which is a very scarce resource; there's simply not enough of it to govern all the decisions leaders are called on to make. This is true for everyone, but particularly for school leaders. A simple review of any of the published school leadership standards suggests that the magnitude of decision-making responsibility on school and district leaders far exceeds the capacity to consistently engage in *System 2* thinking.

The position of the superintendent, for example has become increasingly complex. According to Lytle and Sokoloff,[7] in their article, "A Complex Web: The New Normal for Superintendents," the superintendent position has changed dramatically over the last several decades. In their networking sessions with superintendents they construct a complexity map and describe these changes from both a personal and system level: "What struck us in constructing the map is how many parts of it are relatively recent additions to the superintendent's work. For example, not long ago, office secretaries answered the phone; now the superintendent carries a cell phone and answers from anywhere at anytime."

The new reality is clear; the position of school leader is no longer conducive to the slow, logical, and more deliberate decision-making that *System 2* affords. No one person has the cognitive energy to attend to all of the issues and decisions that are considered to be "part of the job"—*so what does this mean for our organizations and communities?* We will explore these questions and what leaders can do to ensure better decision-making in their organizations in the next chapter.

Questions for Further Reflection

1. Consider the decisions that you have made recently; in how many instances did you use *System 1* processing? *System 2*?

2. Reflect on a time when you felt good about a decision you made using *System 1* processing. Then do the same for *System 2* processing.
3. When does using *System 1* processing make sense? *System 2*?
4. Reflect on the biases and filters discussed in the chapter; which ones resonate most with you? Think of a time when you demonstrated bias.
5. What can you do to help decision-makers within your district become more aware of biases that impact their decisions?

Chapter Five

Frames That Guide Decision-Making

Wisdom is intelligence in context. —Raheel Farooq

In the last chapter we explored *System 1* and *System 2* thinking and other psychological and neurological factors that influence our decision-making. In this chapter we will begin to explore what these discoveries mean for organizational decision-making and introduce conceptual frames to assist leaders in constructing meaning within their context.

Justin Fox,[1] in the article "From Economic Man to Behavioral Economics," describes three primary schools of thought in his historical review of decision-making in organizations. Each school of thought related to decision-making in organizations has held a certain level of prominence historically and when they are examined collectively suggest that decisions within organizations are typically made in one of the following three ways:

- *Heuristics (rules of thumb) and biases*—this is currently believed to be the most prevalent.
- *Going entirely on intuition*, which is often referred to as "going with your gut."
- *Engaging in a more formalized process of decision-analysis* (formulating a problem, listing the possible courses of action, systematically assessing each option).

Each *way of deciding* is used by leaders in a wide array of circumstances at different points in time. The leader models decision-making practices and typically shapes them for the organization. For these reasons it is important to be both aware of the different *ways of deciding (including the impact of bias)* and be intentional in assessing what *way* will be most effective at a given time. The Decision-Making Profile tools in the resource section are designed to help you audit and assess the ways you make decisions.

LEADERSHIP FRAMES

Understanding the *way* in which decisions are made is important. Equally important is *how* the leader thinks about, understands, and defines the context for decision-making. Building on the perspective that educational leadership positions are situated within "a complex web" (from chapter 4), how a leader prioritizes and frames the issues related to decision-making directly impacts how thoughtful and effective an organization is in its response. There are many helpful frames or lenses from which to view and understand organizations and the work of leaders, but it is critical that the leader be constantly open to the *active pursuit of receiving or discovering new conceptual frameworks* as well.

Lee Bolman and Terrence Deal have popularized the practice of *reframing* as an essential leadership behavior.[2] In so doing they have emphasized the notion that key leadership frames, or mental maps, are both "windows on a territory and tools for navigation."

According to Bolman and Deal, each frame tells its own story about organizations. They identify the following four frames and their significance in helping leaders better understand their organizations:

- *Structural*—Focuses on the architecture of the organization—the design of units, subunits, rules, roles, and policies that shape and channel decisions and activities.
- *Human Resources*—Emphasizes an understanding of people with their strengths, weaknesses, emotions, desires, and fears.
- *Political*—Sees organizations as competitive arenas characterized by scarce resources, competing interests, and struggles for power and advantage.
- *Symbolic*—Focuses on issues of meaning and faith. It puts ritual, story, ceremony, play, and culture at the heart of organizational life.[3]

Each frame helps the leader see the organization and the problems and opportunities that need to be addressed in different ways. Even though leaders may have a *preferred* frame that is most consistent with how they see themselves in relation to their organizations, a critical competency for all leaders is the ability to constantly "reframe." In other words, the ability to shift from one frame to another helps leaders redefine situations so they become understandable and manageable.

COMPLEXITY AS A LEADERSHIP FRAMEWORK

In the article, "A Leader's Framework for Decision-Making,"[4] Snowden and Boone offer another framework for thinking specifically about decision-making. Their "Cynefin framework" can help educational leaders see things from new viewpoints, assimilate complex concepts, and address real-world problems and opportunities within their districts and communities. According to the authors, "Cynefin, is a Welsh word that signifies the multiple factors in our environment and our experience that influence us in ways we can never understand."

The Cynefin framework helps leaders determine the prevailing operative context so that they can make appropriate choices. Each domain within the framework requires different actions. In essence, the framework sorts the issues facing leaders into five contexts defined by the *nature of the relationship between cause and effect*. Four of these contexts—*obvious*, *complicated*, *complex*, and *chaotic* require leaders to diagnose situations and to act in contextually appropriate ways. The fifth context, labeled "disorder"—applies when it is unclear which of the other four contexts is predominant.

Adapted from the authors, the following paragraphs offer a brief description of each context.

Obvious Contexts: The Domain of Best Practices

Obvious contexts (formerly referred to as simple) are characterized by stability and clear cause-and-effect relationships that are easily discernible by everyone. Often, the right answer is clear. The context may be technical in nature and not subject to significant change. Decisions in these areas are typically not questioned because all parties share a common understanding. In school district life, these areas include adherence to negotiated agreements, board policies, administrative procedures, and so on. These *obvious* contexts, when properly assessed, require straightforward management and monitoring. In these contexts, leaders assess the facts of the situation, categorize them, and then base their response on established practice.

A seemingly obvious context is not always obvious; however, problems can arise when issues are incorrectly classified within this domain, and in essence are "oversimplified." Leaders must be wary of accepting too little information or evidence from their team, not asking enough questions, or acquiring only the abbreviated or condensed version that ignores the messiness or complexity of the problem or situation. As we discussed in the previous chapter, when working within the *obvious* domain, leaders are also susceptible to all the biases that result from the automatic responses inherent in *System 1* thinking.

In addition, leaders can become complacent when things appear to be going smoothly and miss critical clues that the context is changing. This can happen quickly in schools if leaders do not constantly seek to assess and adapt to changing demographics, technological advances, reform efforts, political sensibilities, and so on. The authors stress that the most frequent collapses into chaos occur because success has bred complacency.

Complicated Contexts: The Domain of Experts

Complicated contexts, unlike obvious ones, may contain multiple right answers, and though there is a clear relationship between cause and effect, not everyone can see it. This is the realm of "known unknowns." Leaders in a complicated context must sense, *analyze*, and respond. This approach is not easy and often requires the expertise of others. For example, an educational leader with a growing student enrollment needs to figure out how to find more physical space for students. To assist in the process, she may use demographers, realtors, architects, designers, technology experts, public relations personnel, and so on to analyze a wide array of data and investigate several options—many of which may be excellent. With many possible options the process is complicated and requires analysis and understanding of consequences at multiple levels.

Narrow thinking is a danger in complicated contexts, too, but it is the experts (rather than the leaders) who are prone to it, and they tend to dominate the domain. When this problem occurs, innovative suggestions by nonexperts may be overlooked or dismissed, resulting in lost opportunities. For example, an architect who has designed many school facilities may have strong preferences about what the library should look like—whereas a community member or other "nonexpert" who observes students studying in the local coffee shops may question the purpose of building a school library (or perhaps any new physical space) at all—perhaps hoping for a more blended learning approach to instruction. It is important for the leader to listen to the experts while simultaneously welcoming novel thoughts and solutions from others.

Another potential obstacle in complicated contexts is "analysis paralysis," where a group hits a stalemate, unable to agree on any answers because of each individual's limited or narrow thinking or sometimes just because the deliberation seems safer and more comfortable than taking action. This is a common problem in school leadership, where continued study may seem more palatable than making politically controversial decisions.

Reaching decisions in the complicated domain can often take a lot of time, and there is always a trade-off between finding a right answer (often from many options) and simply making a timely decision.

Complex Contexts: The Domain of Emergence

In the complicated context, it may take a while to get there, but there is always at least one right answer. Within the complex context, the realm of "unknown knowns," however, there is not one right answer, because things are in constant flux. This is the most common domain for organizational life today, including schools. Most situations and decisions in organizations are complex, because the organizational context is constantly changing. For example, the widespread use of social media (twenty-four hours a day, seven days a week) has made what once may have been complicated scenarios increasingly "complex." A colleague shared a story about a demographer sharing data at a board meeting that suggested the likelihood of some enrollment challenges in the future. Before the meeting ended a parent group had activated a website titled "save our school" and provoked others in a social media war around issues of privilege, social economic status, and race. For the leaders, identifying and defining the nature of the "problem" became increasingly multifaceted and complex.

That is why the authors recommend when in the complex domain, *instead of attempting to impose a course of action, leaders must patiently allow the path forward to reveal itself. They need to probe first, then sense, and then respond.*

As in the other contexts, leaders face several challenges in the complex domain. Of primary concern is the temptation to fall back into traditional management styles—to employ "tried and true" plans with defined outcomes when they do not quickly achieve the results they were aiming for. If they try to over-control the organization, however, they will preempt the opportunity for informative patterns to emerge. *Leaders who try to impose order in a complex context will fail, but those who set the stage, step back a bit, allow patterns to emerge, and determine which ones are desirable will succeed.* With patient and thoughtful leadership this domain affords schools great opportunities for creativity, discovery, and innovation to flourish.

Chaotic Contexts: The Domain of Rapid Response

In a chaotic context, leaders don't search for the right answer, because the relationships between cause and effect are shifting constantly and no manageable patterns exist. This is the realm of "unknowables." Crises and emergencies fall into this category. In the chaotic domain, a leader's immediate job is not to discover patterns, but instead to establish order and stability. *The decision approach is to act—sense—and respond.* A leader must first act to establish order, then sense where stability is present, and then respond by working to transform the situation from chaos to complexity, where the identification of emerging patterns can both help prevent future crises and discern new opportunities. Typically the leader needs to communicate directly, immediately, and with authority. These highly directive behaviors that work well in a crisis situation, however, are generally not effective in other leadership contexts.

DISORDER

The very nature of the fifth context—*disorder*—when experiencing it is particularly difficult to recognize. Here, multiple perspectives jostle for prominence and the leader is unable to identify which of the other four domains is dominant. The leader continues to gather more information, often relying on more comfortable techniques until more fully understanding how to intervene in a contextually appropriate way.

Conceptual models like the *Cynefin framework* demonstrate the importance of leaders being able to constantly reframe and accurately assess, and adapt to their ever-changing context. Effective leadership is contextual. Leaders need to constantly monitor, assess, and identify their context and then adjust their behaviors and decisions to match that context. In addition, they need to continually *define reality*, within the context they have identified for all members of the school district and community.

Questions for Further Reflection

1. To what extent is each school of thought related to organizational decision-making evidenced in your school or district?
2. What organizational frames are you most comfortable with? Least comfortable with?
3. To what extent and in what ways do you engage in the practice of "reframing"?
4. In considering your context how easily and frequently are decisions categorized as obvious, complicated, complex, or chaotic?
5. In what ways are frameworks helpful in understanding, defining, and communicating "reality" in your school or district?

III

Do

The third section examines what leaders *do* to establish the conditions for effective decision-making including how they employ or implement organizational decisions. This section is focused on *leader actions*, including building capacity, designing a decision-friendly organizational architecture, employing and assessing decision-making models, and processing and enacting decisions.

Chapter 6 specifically addresses how leaders build capacity for decision-making in their organizations through creating, developing, and sustaining productive teams and social networks.

Chapter 7 explores how leaders design and shape the environments in which they lead by discussing the ways in which leaders comprehensively build the architecture for organizational decision-making. These ways include: thinking differently about the work; engaging in leadership behaviors that establish the conditions for effective decision-making; defining and assessing decision quality; and embracing social exploration and idea flow.

In chapter 8 the focus shifts to the decision-making process itself and how leaders *decide how to decide.* The discussion introduces possible models for leaders to employ in different scenarios that help them address how to act thoughtfully, strategically, and decisively as problem-solvers.

Chapter 9 highlights the importance of defining the problem correctly and offers suggestions on how leaders can begin to address the issue of *problem definition* by asking the right questions, challenging assumptions, and insisting on evidence-focused conversations.

Finally, chapter 10 addresses the importance of effectively enacting decisions. Effective decision-making practices for leaders do not end with making the decision. Leaders must also act to *manage the consequences of decisions and to create and support the conditions to ensure the desired results.* This chapter will discuss what leaders can personally and organizationally do to improve their decision-making practices and use the important *work of making decisions* as leverage for change.

Chapter Six

Building Capacity

Teams and Networks

Alone we can do so little, together we can do so much. —Helen Keller

In the first five chapters we discussed the importance of knowing self, knowing others, knowing our context, recognizing the forces that shape our decisions, and understanding how we think about and frame our work. In this chapter we shift focus from what leaders *know* and *think*, to what they *do*. We discuss the importance of leaders building capacity for decision-making by focusing on social networks and creating, developing, and sustaining productive teams.

The very nature of an organization suggests the coming together of people to work toward a common mission. School leaders are very tuned into the concept of coming together. We assess our workplace satisfaction and overall climate based in large part on how positive we feel about our relationships. We work with boards, associations, councils, committees, learning communities, groups, and teams as a part of our daily routine—but how often do we think about whether our *coming together* is truly effective?

Organizational theorists have long asserted that the world has become far too complex to ever rely on individuals alone to accomplish our tasks. Collaborative efforts that bring together diverse thoughts and skills are essential to all organizations. Some of these efforts to bring people together are intentional and others occur more naturally.

For example, leaders must never underestimate the power of social networks in influencing behavior. In the book *Connected: The Surprising Power of Our Social Networks*, scientists Christakis and Fowler state,[1] "the key to understanding people is understanding the ties between them." In essence, a network of humans has a special kind of life of its own. A *social network* (that one personally identifies with) is a kind of super-organization that grows and evolves and allows us to understand our actions, choices, and experiences in a new light, and in so doing also influences our decisions.

Within a social network, the "opinion leaders" play a particularly important role of filtering and interpreting issues for their family, friends, and colleagues. For example, an analysis of political networks supports the idea that *where you stand on issues depends on where you sit.* Understanding social networks has tremendous implications for leaders who grapple with how to influence others and understand their receptiveness or resistance to change. We are just beginning to appreciate the great power of social networks and the opportunities leaders have to shape the conditions and structures to ethically and positively influence organizational decision-making.

Most importantly researchers agree that bringing people together thoughtfully and intentionally to collaborate and learn from one another improves educational practice. Michael Fullan has long asserted that teamwork is essential *to situating educators and students as the central driving force in all educational reform efforts.*[2] So given the importance of teams, how do leaders build organizational capacity by inspiring and ensuring effective teamwork? When taking on this challenge, like with almost every leadership act, leaders need to begin by defining and clarifying their purpose and processes.

School leaders frequently use the term "team" as a descriptor when bringing people together, but in reality all groups are not teams. For example, *I often referred to my assistant superintendents and central office administrators as "my team"—other common references included the fourth grade team, the student services team, the data team, and of course the many unique names from our middle school—that actually engaged in the structural practice of "teaming."* In reality, many of these loosely coupled groups would not technically meet the definition of team.

It is important, however, to be precise in our use of terminology if we want to better understand how collective relationships and entities influence and shape decision-making. When leaders use more precise language they are better able to appropriately identify purposes, expectations, and protocols for all groups and design collective experiences for more effective decision-making.

So let's begin with a definition. *What is a team?* In their historically significant article, "The Discipline of Teams,"[3] Katzenbach and Smith define a team as "a small number of people with complementary skills who are committed to a common purpose, set of performance goals, and approach for which they hold themselves mutually accountable."

So simply stated the following four elements—*common commitment and purpose*, *performance goals*, *complementary skills*, and *mutual accountability* are fundamental to distinguishing a functioning team from other groups.

But not all teams are the same. To help us consider differences the authors classify teams into three varieties—*teams that recommend things*, *teams that make or do things*, and *teams that run things*.

Focusing more explicitly on action over time, Susan Wheelan, author of *Creating Effective Teams*,[4] describes the difference between workgroups and teams along an evolving continuum. She contends that a workgroup becomes a team "when shared goals have been established and effective methods to accomplish those goals are in place. Members of high performance teams feel engaged, committed, and valued."

Workgroups and teams evolve and function effectively when they are planted within a positive organizational climate where capacity building is a way of life. In other words, the organization provides a compelling context in which teams are able to experience what Daniel Pink and others describe as essential ingredients to motivation—*autonomy*, *mastery*, and *purpose*.

High-performing teams are productive and valuable in any organization. In schools, like most organizations, a significant portion of the work is conducted by workgroups and teams; therefore, it is essential that school leaders understand how to grow and sustain their value. The messages and actions sent from the leader greatly impact the experience of teams and whether they flourish or fail. *The leader shapes the culture of the organization and organizational cultures impact team effectiveness.*

Susan Wheelan describes eight principles embedded within the organizational culture that encourages high-team performance.[5] The following eight paragraphs briefly discuss these principles from the perspective of what school leaders should do.

Leaders should *clearly define the organization's mission*. Groups and teams need to understand the mission of the district or school and the team's role within the organization. When leaders bring people together they must energize them around the shared vision and be clear and explicit in addressing the following: *What specific purpose does the team serve in supporting our greater mission?*

Effective leaders *support innovation*. Bringing people together with diverse perspectives can foster exceptional creativity, but unless the greater organization supports it (as modeled by leaders) team members will quickly become dispirited and discouraged. Far too often in schools, team members generate powerful ideas that get lost or attacked when shared district-wide or with administrators. How often have you heard the following? *We tried that before and it didn't work*, or *we can't get that through the teachers' union*, or *the board will never go for that*. If we want our organizations to truly benefit from the power of teams, leaders need to inspire teamwork that challenges the status quo—not defends it.

Leaders passionately and consistently *expect success*. Leaders have a responsibility to communicate that they believe in the power and efficacy of the team and that they expect it to be successful in carrying out its work. This requires that educational leaders are thoughtful about the number, nature, diverse composition, and purpose of their teams and workgroups and are prepared to support them both symbolically and with the resources that they need to be successful.

Leaders explicitly communicate that they *value superior quality and service*. Along with expecting success, leaders should expect teams to produce high-quality work and hold them accountable for doing so. To ensure this happens, quality performance indicators need to be established before the teamwork begins and monitored and assessed throughout the process.

Leaders also *pay attention to detail and structural issues*. Leaders have the responsibility to be clear and explicit about what it takes to be successful. Too often in schools, we initiate new committees, councils, task forces, and so on without providing a thoughtful, detailed description of the purpose, scope of the work, relationship to other working groups, and the expectations and parameters for decision-making.

In one small district (following an outcry from teachers and administrators of feeling over-extended), we conducted an audit of the wide array of workgroups and committees we had in place. We discovered that we had over thirty groups, often with competing purposes, that continued to meet on a regular basis. This exhaustive and ineffective structure drained time, energy, and other resources from both the participants and the district. Over time, the loosely coupled structure continued to expand because (regardless of their effectiveness) people had become "owners" of their groups and committed to their preservation. So each time a new initiative was introduced a new committee was formed.

Leaders demonstrate that they *value team recommendations*. Leaders invoke trust and engagement when they are honest about processes and outcomes. All workgroups and teams must be clear about their purposes and the processes through which their work will be received and absorbed into the organization. Group members should not expect that their work recommendations will be automatically accepted, but it is critical that they understand from the onset what the processes and decision protocols are relative to the receipt of their work. If this is not established at the onset there is a strong likelihood that there will be unmet expectations and discouragement on the part of team members. When group recommendations are not valued, groups and individuals throughout the organization become cynical about how serious the leader is about soliciting input.

Leaders *set clear expectations for group output, quality timing, and pacing*. Leaders need to work closely with team leaders in developing and establishing expectations, parameters, quality indicators, timeline benchmarks, and deadlines. A constant communication loop is essential to ensure that the team has the training, resources, and authority it needs to be successful.

Leaders publicly and personally *reward teamwork.* It is common in many organizations to link team performance to compensation, but this is not a widespread practice in schools. It is certainly possible, however, for school leaders to more formally emphasize the importance of professional collaboration and teamwork by explicitly making teamwork a part of the teacher and administrator supervision and evaluation process. In addition, school leaders can stress the importance of team contributions over individual efforts in more subtle ways through the consistent use of words and actions that demonstrate that they genuinely value the contributions of the team. Ultimately however, leaders most effectively communicate the value of teamwork by giving their workgroups and teams meaningful tasks and the resources they need to do their best.

Frequently educational leaders work under the assumption that *if we just bring good people together they will work productively.* This is not the case. In addition to an organizational culture that values and supports teamwork, leaders need to intentionally set up the conditions for teams and workgroups to be successful.

ORGANIZATIONAL CONDITIONS FOR EFFECTIVE TEAMWORK

The following paragraphs highlight the organizational conditions for productive and effective teamwork. It is the responsibility of the leader to ensure that these four conditions are in place.

First and foremost, teams need *meaningful and purposeful work that requires continuous learning, knowledge sharing, and interdependence.* Leaders do not want to delegate technical work (or decisions that warrant simple or obvious responses) to a team that could be easily done by an individual.

Second, the leader needs to ensure that the personnel assigned to a team have the capacity to *meaningfully engage in productive teamwork.* The selection of team members must not be a personality contest or who has the most "seniority" mandate. Members should be selected based on their knowledge, skills, diverse perspectives, and their potential for becoming an excellent team member.

When committees or groups are formed in schools there is often an entitlement expectation—*I have been in the job the longest, so I should be on the committee.* Longevity does not ensure an effective team member. There are a lot of factors to consider in team selection, but perhaps most importantly effective team members demonstrate a commitment to the goals of the group, an appreciation of the team process, and an investment to group performance over individual recognition.

Third, leaders ensure that team members receive *the training and resources they need to be successful.* Unfortunately, this critical need is often not addressed in schools. Allocating the time for team members to meet specific to the team task is itself a huge challenge (especially when carved out of student time) and finding additional time for training may feel like overkill or seem "excessive," but it is not. School personnel at all levels spend a tremendous amount of time "meeting." To ensure that meeting time is productive and meaningful, leaders need to prepare and equip their people to work together in meaningful ways. In preparation for their work, team members should receive training in everything from basic group processes and the evolution of teams, to specific meeting protocols. When teams are working, leaders need to constantly monitor and support the team's operational needs. Doing so often requires providing access to a wide array of people and data.

Finally, leaders need to demonstrate *visible support and ensure the integration of organizational learning*. It goes without saying that leaders need to *walk their talk* and visibly support and validate team efforts. Part of doing so requires the deep integration of teamwork and learning in ways that systematically impact organizational learning and growth. Not only do leaders want the team to continually grow and evolve, they want to ensure that the team itself has the capacity to impact organizational learning. Everyone should benefit from the team.

DELEGATING DECISIONS

We have reviewed cultural and leadership behaviors that contribute to team effectiveness and appreciate that teams and workgroups are venues for much of the adult work and learning in schools. Therefore, either implicitly or explicitly, teams play a significant role in decision-making and problem-solving in our complex organizations. *So when and how do leaders delegate decision-making to teams?*

As is the case with leaders in any complex organization, delegation and the distribution of leadership responsibilities is essential to organizational progress. As we discussed previously, there are many positives associated with engaging teams in meaningful work. It is important to remember that it is the responsibility of the leader to ensure that the purpose of the workgroup or team is well articulated and positioned within the district and that the participants are well prepared to take on the work that is assigned to them.

As previously noted, leaders routinely engage workgroups and teams in their schools for a wide array of reasons. District and school personnel meet (with constituency groups) to inform and solicit input on pressing issues, to address resource allocation constraints, to plan and lead change initiatives, to negotiate contracts, to routinely discuss working conditions among representatives from the association and administration, to assess and evaluate progress and programs, to assess student performance data, to map curriculum, to learn together in professional learning communities, and the list goes on and on.

As the list suggests, workgroups and teams serve very different purposes in school districts; it is therefore essential that leaders are *fundamentally clear about each group's purpose and decision-making potential, authority, and responsibilities*.

The extent of authority for decisions needs to be critically and thoughtfully determined and communicated by the school or district leader.

When it comes to delegation decisions, there are many models that provide insights and tools for leaders. According to the Hoy-Tarter assessment,[6] in making the determination to delegate to a team the leader should begin by thoughtfully reflecting on the following critical questions related to *relevance*, *expertise*, and *trust*:

- *Do the team members have a personal stake in the outcomes of the decision? (the relevance question)*
- *Do the team members have the expertise to make a knowledgeable contribution? (the expertise question)*
- *Can you trust the team to make a decision in the best interest of the organization? (the trust question)*

In addition, within the broader context of relevance, expertise, and trust the educational leader should further consider:

- The level or extent of "buy-in" that is needed for the decision to be implemented.
- The context and nature of the decision. What is the level of complexity? Is the decision or problem to be solved technical or adaptive in nature?
- What data or evidence is available and accessible to the team?
- What is the degree of trust, credibility, and value of the team by the organization, constituent groups, and public arbiters?
- What implications does delegation have for the desired environment/climate and long-term relationship within the school or community?
- How does the Board of Education perceive and accept the team process and accountability?
- What is the likelihood of being able to "live with" recommendations or decisions? What are the risks and to whom?

Deciding who to include in the decision-making process and how much influence to give them over the final outcome can be difficult and controversial. Leaders want to delegate appropriately but not overburden teams with "simplistic" efforts that are not a meaningful and productive use of team time, expertise, and resources. Boudett and City in their book,[7] *Meeting Wise*, indicate that finding time for people to come together is typically a priority in schools, but that leaders also need to regularly assess if the time they have is being used wisely. The authors provide a formula to estimate the annual (financial) investment in a meeting. Essentially "you multiply the number of people at the meeting by the number of hours in the meeting by the average hourly earnings of the people in the meeting by the number of meetings per year."[8]

Carefully considering the financial costs of meeting time and weighing all that was previously discussed, *finding the right balance* when delegating decision-making in a school district is essential. Ultimately, the leader's act of delegation can have significant repercussions, for both the quality of the decision and the team's and organization's morale, motivation, and sense of efficacy.

Questions for Further Reflection

1. What workgroups do you have in your district? What teams?
2. In what ways is teamwork explicitly supported in the organization? Not adequately supported?
3. To what extent are you comfortable with the number of groups, and the shared understanding of their purpose?
4. In what ways can you improve the level of productivity and quality of work of your teams?
5. How do you delegate decisions to teams and workgroups? Are you effective in your delegation efforts? How do you know?

Chapter Seven

Building the Architecture for Decision-Making

> Leaders set the context and create the conditions in which individuals and organizations thrive. —Bob Anderson

The first several chapters of the book focus on knowing and building capacity in ourselves and the people with whom we work and serve. If leaders constantly strive to understand and improve their leadership practices by building strong teams and working in ways that foster high levels of engagement and ownership in others they lay the foundation for effective decision-making—but that alone is not sufficient.

In this chapter we discuss ways school leaders can comprehensively build the architecture for organizational decision-making by thinking differently about the work, engaging in leadership behaviors that establish the conditions for effective decision-making, defining and assessing decision quality, and by embracing social exploration and idea flow. In essence, this chapter will explore how leaders design and shape the environments in which they lead.

Our focus is on what leaders can do to design organizational environments that are conducive to effective decision-making, but it is important to acknowledge that leaders also have the ability to influence by design the *actual choices and decisions* of people within their organizations. This is often referred to as *choice architecture*. According to Richard Thaler and Cass Sunstein, authors of the book, *Nudge: Improving Decisions about Wealth, Health and Happiness,*[1] there are many parallels between choice architecture and more traditional forms of architecture. Of greatest significance is that in both forms of architecture there is *no such thing as a "neutral" design.* They cite as an example, that where bathrooms and stairways are placed in a building can impact how people interact. Small and apparently insignificant details can have major impacts on people's choices and behaviors. Given this, a good rule of thumb is to assume that "everything matters."

Having introduced the concept of *choice architecture*, and the tremendous opportunity leaders have to influence the choices people make, we also have to emphasize the ethical responsibility leaders have that is fundamental to their positional power. Leaders act as role models, who consistently communicate the importance of ethical standards and hold people accountable to those standards. So our underlying assumption throughout this discussion is that *the foundation to an effective decision-making architecture is an ethical environment in which others work and learn*. So when the term architecture is used within this book, it is used with a focus on *designing the conditions for effective decision-making organizationally*, not on efforts to directly influence the direction of those decisions.

In building the architecture for effective decision-making the leader needs to he highly focused and intentional in his efforts. In their article, *An Organization-Wide Approach to Good Decision Making*,[2] Larry Neal and Carl Spetzler emphasize the importance of a rigorous organization-wide approach to decision-making. They argue that without an explicit and transparent approach that is practiced consistently throughout the organization, "the organization is at the mercy of the biggest bias of all: the perception that it is good at making decisions." The leader is responsible for ensuring that not only are the conditions for effective decision-making nurtured and sustained, but also that the organizational-wide approach is widely understood and consistently practiced.

DECISION-MAKING AS THE WORK ITSELF

Tom Davenport, in his article, "The Big Lesson from 12 Good Decisions,"[3] suggests that a significant way to improve decision-making in organizations is to begin with thinking about the act of decision-making itself. It is typical for leaders to think about decision-making as a routine act that is separate from the "real work." In other words, decision-making occurs in order for the real work in the organization to proceed. But if leaders are able to shift their thinking and consider decision-making as the *work itself*, they will place a much greater significance on this routine leadership act, and give it the intentionality, leverage, and focus it requires.

This simple shift in perspective means that leaders approach decision-making throughout the organization with *the same level of discipline and focus that they bring to other areas.* With this new perspective, leaders will grow to appreciate the power of decision-making as a significant lever to move their organizations forward and understand that decisions improve when the right people, tools, and processes are consistently employed.

In other words, when leaders view decision-making as the *work itself* they realize that many general principles about managing good work apply to it. Within this context, Davenport offers five guidelines for leaders when engaging in decision-making work:[4]

- *Don't do all the decision work yourself.*
- *Bring a big toolkit to your decision work.*
- *Measure before deciding.* Use data and analytics extensively and thoughtfully.
- *Systematically review your work.* Decisions will get better if you establish the habit of reviewing them after the fact.
- *Have a process for decision work.* Processes for decision-making should be transparent, contextually relevant, thoughtfully selected, employed, and evaluated.

These principles can be applied to all areas of school leadership. For example, when working on school improvement efforts, leaders often focus initially on structural issues. These are typically the most visible actions and they seem most obvious. The thinking goes something like this: *If we restructure our central office, further extend the length of the school day, change the organizational chart, or rework the class schedule we will be more effective.* The reality is that rarely do structural changes alone have a significant impact on improving student learning or on the overall performance of the school district.

When we shift perspective and think about decision-making as the *work itself*, the focus is not so much about *restructuring* our organizations as it is about our capacity to *structure our organizations for the essential work of effective decision-making.* The design challenge for leaders therefore is to *structure* school districts so that all members can individually and collectively make strategic decisions that leverage the organization for high-quality continuous learning and performance over time.

DECISION QUALITY

School leaders, when defining *decision-making as the work itself*, have considerable power and influence in shaping the conditions that are conducive to effective decision-making. An important step in designing the structure or architecture for good organizational decision-making is determining *what a good decision looks like.* Neal and Spetzler suggest that an effective way to define and measure a "good decision" is through the use of a *Decision*

Quality (DQ) assessment.[5] The authors identify and describe the following six elements of decision quality that characterize any high-quality decision.

- *An appropriate frame*, including a clear understanding of the problem and what needs to be achieved.
- *Creative, doable alternatives* from which to choose the one likely to achieve the most of what you want.
- *Meaningful information* that is reliable, unbiased, and reflects all relevant uncertainties and intangibles.
- *Clarity about desired outcomes*, including acceptable trade-offs.
- *Solid reasoning and sound logic* that includes considerations of uncertainty and insight at the appropriate level of complexity.
- *Commitment to action by all stakeholders* necessary to achieve effective action.

The decision quality assessment can be a very helpful tool (see resource section) when used both proactively before a decision is made and as an evaluation tool to assess the effectiveness of a decision. Since decisions are always made within a context, school leaders may find it helpful to reflect on the following broader contextual questions as well, when assessing decision quality:

1. *Do we know where we are, where we are going, and what we are trying to accomplish?* We discussed the importance of having a vision and clear sense of purpose in chapter 3. In assessing decision quality, it is important to consider it within this critical context—*What do the data tell us about our current reality? How does the decision we are assessing align with our values and mission and further advance our vision?*
2. *Are we using the right drivers*? Michael Fullan discusses the importance of being focused on the right *drivers*.[6] In other words, the drivers that are going to have the most impact on advancing our work. Fullan describes the best drivers are ones that*: Foster intrinsic motivation of teachers and students; Engage educators and students in continuous improvement of instruction and learning; Inspire collective or team work; and Affect all teachers and students.*
3. *Have we considered our situation from a variety of organizational frames?* When we assess the quality of the decision it is important to do so using multiple frames. Bolman and Deal argue the importance of constantly reframing through the fluid use of the *political, structural, human resource*, and *symbolic frames*.[7] To what extent have we "reframed" or added new conceptual frames to our leadership repertoire?

4. *What is the level of complexity?* In chapter 5 we discussed the *Cynefin framework* for assessing the level of complexity. Were the problem and ultimate decision appropriately identified as *obvious, complicated, complex, chaotic,* or *disorder?*
5. *What is our personal understanding of the degree of change needed?* What evidence/data do we have about our current reality? Since decisions are actions they move us in a particular direction. As we assess the quality of our decisions it is important to consider the evidence or gap analysis between our current reality and the vision we have for our schools. What level of change do we believe is necessary in our districts? Do the decision process and outcome support that level of change? For example, is the change needed *evolutionary/transactional* (incremental steps to fix a problem or fix part of a system) or *revolutionary/transformational* (a jolt to the system, where nothing will be the same again)? Does the decision address the potential for organizational change that is *reactive* (made in response to a significant event/situation/crisis) or *anticipatory* (made in anticipation of future needs)?
6. *How do we perceive our role and the roles of others in leading change and ensuring equity and social justice?* In assessing the quality of our organizational decisions what role are we playing as leader? Are we critiquing our organizational decisions as *agents of change* or as *managers of the status quo?*
7. *Do the decisions meet our ethical standards?* The following questions adapted from the *Josephson Institute of Ethics* can serve as a guide for personal reflection in assessing the ethical quality of the decision.[8]

   - *Does the decision conflict with any core ethical values?*
   - *How does the decision affect others?*
   - *Are the actions legal?*
   - *How would the decision look if it were reported on the news or in another public forum?*
   - *How would reasonable people perceive the decision?*
   - *Can you rationally and honestly defend the decision?*

In addition to ensuring that all decisions are ethical and socially just, it is important that leaders make certain that they give voice to others in the decision-making process. Leaders need to delegate thoughtfully and strategically, and remember that when people feel acted upon and have little or no voice or control in the process, dissatisfaction, frustration, and alienation are common responses to the resulting decisions.

SOCIAL EXPLORATION AND IDEA FLOW

School leaders can also shape the organizational architecture for decision-making by *ensuring conditions that support social exploration and idea flow.* Good decisions don't happen in a vacuum. They happen when people learn from and draw on the experiences of others. This type of learning can have long-term, positive implications for decision-making in schools. In the article, "Beyond the Echo Chamber,"[9] Pentland contends that the best decisions result from constant social exploration—*the process of gathering, winnowing, and testing out ideas from other people.* Social exploration works well when the sources of ideas are diverse and independent and the decision maker is able to successfully tap into the "wisdom of the crowd."

Researchers have found that social explorers spend enormous amounts of time searching for new people and ideas—not necessarily just the best people and ideas. By forming connections with a wide array of people and gaining exposure to many different perspectives they are able to bounce the potentially most promising ideas off other people to see which ones resonate. *Generally, those ideas are micro-strategies—examples of actions that might be taken, circumstances conducive to the action, and possible outcomes.* Then, by assembling a great set of micro-strategies, social explorers can make better decisions.

Pentland further addresses how social exploration fosters better problem-solving over time. He found from research that the best problem-solvers engaged in

> "preparatory exploration"—that is, they proactively developed relationships and connections with other experts and later tapped them for help with completing critical tasks. Moreover, the social networks of the star performers were more diverse than the networks of the middling performers. Middling performers saw the world only from the viewpoint of their jobs and limited their social learning to people in similar roles. Stars, on the other hand, reached out to people from a broader set of work roles. . . . Because the stars could see the situation from a variety of viewpoints, they could develop better solutions to problems.[10]

For social exploration to have an impact in schools, leaders must model, foster, and expect all members of the organization to engage in social exploratory behaviors.

In essence, leaders need to ensure that district decision-makers routinely tap into diverse social networks. If the circle of connections is too tight and the members of it are too similar, it is easy to become trapped in an "echo chamber" where the same ideas keep circulating.

The "echo chamber" can be especially problematic in schools, where it is easy to become insulated and isolated. Educators often feel the burden of increased public scrutiny and accountability and when feeling under attack—retreat. They become paralyzed in self-preservation and survivor mode. School district leaders need to resist these behaviors and challenge their people to be more accepting and less dismissive of other perspectives from different sectors. The idea that nobody understands us and that we are so different (and far more honorable) can be limiting. Educators like all professionals need to seek out different perspectives that encourage playful and critical debate over new and often uncomfortable ideas.

It is essential for leaders to model this behavior by looking beyond their own internal networks of educators to outsiders who can serve as critical friends or partners in thought and leader development. Having knowledgeable and trustworthy people outside of the field of education that can challenge status quo practices and offer different perspectives can be invaluable.

Questions for Further Reflection

1. In what ways does thinking about decision-making as the *work itself* impact your daily practice? The practices of others in your organization?
2. What stood out as most significant to you when you conducted a decision quality assessment?
3. How can the use of decision quality assessments improve decision-making in your school or district?
4. In what ways do you engage in "social exploration" as a leader?
5. How would you describe idea flow in your school or district?

Chapter Eight

Deciding How to Decide

Employing Different Models

> In any moment of decision the best thing you can do is the right thing, the next best thing is the wrong thing, and the worst thing you can do is nothing. —Theodore Roosevelt

In previous chapters we discussed the importance of understanding self, others, our content, and our context. We also considered the many factors rational and irrational that influence our decision-making. We reviewed ways to design a more decision-friendly architecture and an action oriented, decision-driven organization. In this chapter we are going to focus on employing models that help leaders address how to act thoughtfully, strategically, and decisively as problem-solvers.

Sometimes the terms decision-making and problem-solving are used interchangeably. For the purposes of this discussion, however, we would like to make a distinction between the two. Leaders make hundreds of decisions during the day (choosing between different alternatives) and many of these decisions as we learned with *System 1 thinking* are somewhat automatic or routine. Problem-solving, on the other hand, *is a more complex and focused process that frequently embeds many decisions along the way, including a decision on how to engage in the act of problem-solving.*

Both decision-making and problem-solving are natural and routine in any leadership position. Whether addressing a crisis situation, solving an immediate, high-stakes problem, supporting a team or staff member who is solving a problem, or discovering new problems to solve, the problems vary widely in scope and complexity, but all have in common the expectation that leaders will resolve them. *Leaders are responsible and held accountable for both the processes and resolutions to current and (often) future problems.*

A quick history of decision-making practices in organizations, as reviewed in chapter 5, suggests that some form of decision analysis is recommended when possible. This is because most leaders believe a rational (to any extent possible) plan of action is preferable to more intuitive and biased responses. This recommendation was based on the long-term acceptance of classical decision-making theory, which assumes that decisions should be rational and that there is one best solution to problems that can be discovered and implemented. In accordance with this model, Hoy and Tarter describe a typical classical model sequence of steps that include:[1]

1. *Problem identification*: Problems are defined as discrepancies between actual and desired outcomes and school leaders monitor school operations to identify problems—that is, to determine when performance falls short of expectations.
2. *Problem diagnosis*: Information related to the nature and origin of the problem is collected and analyzed.
3. *Alternatives*: All the possible solution alternatives or options are developed.
4. *Consequences*: The probable effects of each alternative are considered.
5. *Evaluation*: The alternatives are evaluated in terms of the goals and objectives.
6. *Selection*: The best alternative is selected—that is, the one that maximizes the goals and objectives.
7. *Implementation*: The decision is implemented and evaluated.

In essence, the classical model assumes what Hoy and Tarter refer to as an *optimizing strategy* of decision-making. This strategy is based on classical economic theory *that assumes clear goals, complete information, and the cognitive capacity to analyze the problem.* As discussed in earlier chapters, however, human nature and the uncertainties and complexities of organizational life make "optimizing" an impossible choice; therefore the classical model is really more of an ideal than a description of how decision-makers actually function in schools.

A SATISFICING STRATEGY

Given that the optimizing strategy is unrealistic, how do educational leaders typically make decisions? To address this question, Hoy and Tarter explain that Herbert Simon introduced the strategy of *satisficing.*[2] Simon argues that since school leaders do not have the knowledge, ability, or capacity to maximize in complex situations they instead seek to *satisfice—in other words they continue to look for satisfactory solutions that are "good enough."* The authors argue that in doing so *administrators typically make choices using a simplified picture of reality that accounts only for the factors they consider most important.*

DECISION-MAKING: A CYCLICAL PROCESS

So how can leaders improve their decision-making? Given the challenges of attempting to make decision-making more rational in organizations, leaders can begin by thinking about the process differently. Many researchers agree that *decision-making is not a linear process, but instead a cyclical one*. In other words, decision-making is *dynamic* and often *messy*. It typically solves some problems and creates others. Specific improvements that foster the achievement of the organization's purposes in one area often interfere with those in others. The process, however, usually results in incremental progress, because the experience of solving earlier problems contributes to the search for solutions to later problems.

In the *cyclical decision-making model* espoused by Hoy and Tarter,[3] decision-makers typically go through five sequential steps:

1. Recognize and define the problem.
2. Analyze the difficulties in the existing situation.
3. Establish criteria for a satisfactory solution.
4. Develop a strategy for action, including the specification of possible alternatives, the prediction of probable consequences, deliberation, and the selection of an action plan.
5. Initiate the plan of action.

   - program
   - communicate
   - monitor
   - evaluate

The authors remind us that *although the process is conceived as a sequential pattern in which each step serves as a logical basis for the next, the process is also cyclical.* Thus, decision-making may be entered into at any stage and will occur over and over again.

Decision-making cycles occur simultaneously in our school districts. For example, one highly formalized cycle, related to visioning and goal setting (strategic thinking and planning), may be proceeding at the level of the board of education; while smaller and related sequential cycles, regarding curriculum, instruction, assessment, pupil personnel services, financial management, and facilities planning, may be progressing at the district level; with further related iterations of decision-making at the school sites.

In essence, *it is a complex interaction of events in different areas of the organization that are both tightly and loosely coupled.*

DIFFERENT MODELS

Before pursuing further discussion of different models it is important to reconcile the paradoxical quandary related to the value of seemingly *rational* problem-solving models in an *irrational* world. On the one hand, we recognize the many limitations of these problem-solving models; on the other hand, embracing a conceptual model for problem-solving helps us make sense of our work and enables us to communicate throughout our organizations and communities with much greater transparency. Since thoughtful and strategic thinking and communication is essential for leaders (especially in highly visible political contexts), it is important to have some familiarity with different decision-making and problem-solving models and be able to use and adapt them as necessary.

Initial inquiry into problem-solving reveals a wide array of models and frameworks from virtually every discipline. In considering different models, the leader must first and foremost adhere to professional standards and ethical principles.[4] The leader does so by *committing* to do the right thing irrespective of cost; demonstrating *consciousness* in consistently applying moral convictions to all behavior; and exhibiting *competency* in assessing alternatives and eliminating unethical options.

Grounded in ethical principles, the following are just a small sampling of decision-making or problem-solving models that address different needs and can be helpful in a wide variety of educational scenarios. The first two models represent the more classical and formalized decision analysis philosophy of decision-making while the other two are grounded more in heuristics (rules of thumb) and intuition.

Models for Formal Decision-Making Analysis

The Vroom-Yetton-Jago Decision Model[5] provides a useful framework for identifying the best leadership style to adopt for the situation and decision you are facing. The framework in essence helps answer the question—*Should I make this decision myself or delegate it to others?* The model assumes that autocratic styles work some of the time, highly participative styles work at other times, and various combinations of the two work best in all other circumstances.

Your style and the level of participation you need in making the decision is impacted by the following three main factors: *decision quality*, *subordinate commitment*, and *time constraints*. How you assess the impact of these factors helps you determine the best leadership and decision-making style to use. In this complex model, Vroom-Jago *distinguishes three styles of leadership, and five different processes of decision-making.* The leadership styles include autocratic, consultative, and collaborative. For each leadership style there are decision-making process options listed. This is a particularly helpful approach for a leader to use when trying to determine *how* a decision should be made (or problem solved) and by *whom*.

When working to ensure a continuous process of creative and innovative problem-solving over the long term, the *Simplex Process* is a good option. This process was developed by Min Basadur and is described in detail on the following Applied Creativity website, http://www.basadur.com/howwedoit/an8stepprocess/tabid/82/default.aspx.[6]

This formal approach to creative problem-solving follows an eight-stage continuous cycle. Within each of the following areas, *problem formulation, solution formulation, and solution implementation there are multiple stages.* Upon completion of the eight stages you start it again to find and solve another problem. The process is designed to generate the most creative solutions over time and to help ensure continuous improvement. For the district leader who believes that problems are truly opportunities and wants to ensure that the district organization will continue to grow and innovate the *Simplex Process* is a useful organizational tool.

Models for Decision-Making in High-Pressure Situations

When not pursuing a longer horizon, or having the luxury of time (as is frequently the case) leaders need to rely more on intuition and *rules of thumb* (heuristics) that have been acquired through experience over time. In reality, most decisions in schools are made using some form of a heuristic, such as common sense, an educated guess, or rule of thumb. This is particularly true when making decisions under pressure. The following models help leaders better understand how good decision-making in high pressure and fast moving situations typically unfolds.

Research psychologists Gary Klein, Roberta Calderwood, and Anne Clinton-Cirocco identified the Recognition-Primed Decision (RPD) Process,[7] after studying professionals such as firefighters, emergency medical technicians/paramedics, and nuclear technicians, who routinely make quick, life-or-death decisions. They discovered that other decision-making models were inadequate in explaining how people make good decisions under pressure.

The process highlights the three simple steps that people go through, often subconsciously, when needing to make a quick decision in a high-pressure situation. This process is based on "pattern recognition," and on how we use past experiences of similar situations to influence our decisions.

The three steps include:

- *Experiencing* the situation—Essentially take it all in, listen to what is going on and how it is unfolding.
- *Analyzing* the situation—Consider questions such as: Is this a situation that we've experienced before? Are there familiar patterns that we recognize? Is the situation playing out as we would expect?
- *Implementing* the decision—Take action.

To become adept at this level of decision-making, extensive preparation and practice is necessary. This is why it is important for schools to practice drills and simulations (tornado, fire, lock down, active shooter, etc.). Leaders prepare for future decision-making by becoming *familiar* with these scenarios. They gain important insight when these drills are thoughtfully executed, monitored, and critically evaluated.

OODA Loops as described on the Mind Tools website, https://www.mindtools.com/pages/article/newTED_78.htm, is another more heuristic based decision-making model that emanated from military experience.[8] Former US Air Force Colonel John Boyd developed the model after analyzing the success of the American F-86 fighter plane compared with that of the faster, more easily maneuverable Soviet MIG-15. Boyd discovered that the American plane won more battles because the pilot's field of vision was far superior. As a result, the American pilot could assess the situation better and faster than his opponent and out-maneuver the enemy pilot, who would be put off-balance, wouldn't know what to expect, and would start making mistakes.

Boyd learned that *observing* and *orienting* correctly is key to successful decisions. If these initial steps are flawed, they'll lead you to a flawed decision, and a flawed subsequent action. Similar to the RPD process, the OODA Loop model outlines a four-point decision loop that supports *quick, effective, and proactive* decision-making. The four stages are:

1. *Observe*—Collect current information from as many sources as practically possible. Be aware of unfolding circumstances. The more information you can take in here, the more accurate your perception will be. The kind of questions that need to be asked are:

    - What's happening in the environment that directly affects me?
    - What's happening that indirectly affects me?
    - What's happening that may have residual effects later on?
    - Were my predictions accurate?

- Are there any areas where prediction and reality differ significantly?

2. *Orient*—Analyze the information observed, and use it to update your current reality. Orientation is essentially how you interpret a situation, which then leads directly to your decision. To be effective in your orientation of the situation it is essential that you are self-aware of the biases (some of which we discussed previously) that influence your perceptions. The quicker you understand what's going on, the better. It is important to also recognize that you are constantly reorienting as you observe/experience new information.
3. *Decide*—Determine a course of action. Decisions are really your best guesses, based on the observations you've made and the orientation you're using. As such, they should be considered to be *fluid works-in-progress*. As you keep on cycling through the OODA Loop, and new suggestions keep arriving, these can trigger changes to your decisions and subsequent actions—essentially, you're constantly learning as you continue to cycle through the steps.
4. *Act*—Follow through on your decision. You continue to cycle through the OODA Loop by observing the results of your actions, seeing whether you've achieved the results you intended, reviewing and revising your initial decision, and moving to your next action.

The goal of the model is to increase the speed with which you *orient* and *reorient* based on new information coming in. You want to be able to make a smooth and direct transition between *what you observe, how you interpret it, and what you do about it.* When you make these transitions rapidly, you're in a position to be more nimble, adaptive, and proactive and make changes to your decisions and strategy quickly and decisively. This nimble model can help school leaders prepare for and navigate the daily challenges of an increasingly complex environment that is constantly changing.

Questions for Further Reflection

1. What experiences have you had using a *satisficing* strategy of decision-making?
2. What is your preferred management style? In what ways does your preferred style impact your decision-making?
3. How do you *decide how to decide*? When to make the decision on your own—and when to delegate?
4. Which model of decision-making is most prevalent in your district?
5. How can you prepare your district to be more effective in using heuristic techniques in decision-making?

Chapter Nine

Defining the Problem

> If I were given one hour to save the planet, I would spend 59 minutes defining the problem and one minute resolving it. —Albert Einstein

The one step that is foundational to every problem-solving model is *defining the problem.* Too often leaders expend a tremendous amount of district effort, energy, and resources into solving a problem that has not been sufficiently identified and defined. A lot of precious meeting time is wasted jumping to solutions when the problem itself is not clear. Regardless of whether leaders employ an intuitive, heuristic, or a more formalized and analytical approach, defining the problem accurately is essential to a successful resolution.

In this chapter we will discuss how leaders can begin to address the issue of *problem definition* by asking the right questions, challenging assumptions, and insisting on evidence-focused conversations.

How leaders understand and define problems makes a difference. A quick and narrow definition of the problem can restrict options and treat symptoms, not the real problem. For example, a leader whose district is struggling with getting routine work completed effectively and on time may define the problem as not having enough administrative personnel. When the problem is defined *as too few administrators*, it can only be solved by hiring more administrators. If, on the other hand, the issue is thought about more broadly one might consider other possibilities that could be contributing to unmet work-related expectations. The leader might consider the possibility that the district is taking on too many initiatives and there is a lack of clarity around focus and priorities. Perhaps the existing team is operating in bureaucratic silos and not communicating or collaborating effectively. Maybe administrators are not skilled in efficient practices or lack competency in critical areas.

These are just a few other ways of understanding and defining the problem—all of which would trigger very different solutions.

How leaders interpret and articulate issues for their organizations is also critically important. This is evidenced in the following example related to policy work around improving teacher performance. On a national level there has been extensive policy work focused on teacher accountability, as well as teacher growth and learning. How leaders in an individual district interpret "the problem" that these policy initiatives are intended to address impacts how the district responds. If a district sees the *policy as the "problem"* (now we have to comply with this ridiculous mandate), the opportunity to leverage the policy to enhance teacher learning is lost. If on the other hand, the policy is perceived and communicated as an *opportunity* to create new possibilities that support teachers and enhance the profession—there is unlimited potential.

We know that how a leader defines and adopts *a problem* (defining it within one's own context) has a tremendous impact on how individuals and the organization collectively are able to understand it and move forward in assessing alternatives and generating new possibilities. It is also essential that leaders are transparent and use intentional and targeted communication strategies.

It is through effective communication that leaders *define reality* for their organizations and communities. Leaders understand that one of the best ways to gain leverage is to *shape the conversation.* In school communities where issues are highly politicized—*leaders need to clearly define the problem to be solved.* If they don't, someone else will. Issues that are not clearly defined and articulated in a timely way become open to the likelihood of new, multiple, and competing versions of the problem.

When multiple versions of the problem exist, it becomes extremely difficult for the leader to *define reality*, challenge assumptions, and engage in critically robust and meaningful discourse around solutions. Multiple versions and a lack of clarity related to the nature of the problem can contribute to high levels of frustration and widespread unmet expectations, because everyone is focused on different things. For example, in a tight negotiations process the board and administrators may define *the problem* as simply related to financial compensation, whereas the teachers may see *the problem* as one of personal value and being underappreciated. If the problem is defined and communicated as purely financial, all efforts and communication are directed toward compensation. When this happens, there is little opportunity for the different sides to come together to creatively expand options for addressing work efficacy issues in more holistic ways.

TOOLS AND STRATEGIES

Clearly identifying the problem is essential to effective decision-making and fortunately there are a wide array of tools, strategies, and mental models or approaches available to assist leaders in this effort. The Mind Tools website (https://www.mindtools.com/pages/main/newMN_TMC.htm) is an excellent resource for learning about these tools.[1] The following discussion includes just two examples from a wide array of possibilities highlighted by Mind Tools.

The first is a useful approach to help leaders *expand thinking about the broader issue.* The *CATWOE strategy* was first introduced by researcher David Smyth in 1975 and can be easily adapted to the educational arena.[2] The questions that guide the strategy focus on the following six *CATWOE elements*:

1. *Customers* (students, parents, community)—Who are they and how does the issue affect them?
2. *Actors* (teachers, administrators, etc.)—Who is involved in the situation? Who will be involved in implementing solutions? What will impact their success?
3. *Transformation process*—What systems or processes does the issue impact?
4. *Worldview*—What is the big picture? What are the wider impacts of the issue?
5. *Owners*—Who owns the process or situation under investigation and what role will they play in the solution?
6. *Environmental constraints*—What are the constraints and limitations that will impact the solution and its success?

When a leader or team considers the situation from all six perspectives thinking is expanded and the problem can be defined and addressed more systemically. In other words, a strategy like CATWOE helps the leader gain insight into multiple perspectives related to the bigger issues and far-reaching implications that extend beyond the most visible occurrence of the problem.

Root Cause Analysis Tools are also helpful.[3] The Root Cause Analysis (RCA) is a collective term that describes a wide range of approaches, tools, and techniques that are used to uncover the *causes* of problems. RCA tools are helpful in problem identification because they help leaders get to the deeper issues and avoid the natural inclination to quickly treat the most visible concerns, which are often symptomatic of a larger systemic problem that needs attention.

Root cause analysis assumes that systems and events are interrelated and that an action in one area triggers an action in another. Essentially these tools help leaders answer the questions: *What happened? Why did it happen? What can we do to reduce the likelihood of it happening again?*

One helpful and efficient *RCA* tool for educational leaders is the *five whys technique.* Essentially, when a problem occurs, you uncover its nature and source by asking "why" no fewer than five times until you can discover something that you can impact or control. The following is an example of how the strategy unfolds:

- *Problem:* The Board of Education did not approve the recommended elementary math curriculum

    1. *Why?* Board members indicated they did not have enough evidence to support adopting a new math program.
    2. *Why?* There were no data in the rationale provided that supported a need for changing the current program.
    3. *Why?* The anecdotal rationale did not address the current program; it just emphasized the bells and whistles of the new program.
    4. *Why?* The existing program was not adequately evaluated and a compelling need for a new program communicated.
    5. *Why?* The district does not have an evidence-based program evaluation process in place.

- *Counter measure*—The district needs to develop a formal, evidence-based process for program evaluation.

In using the *five whys* or any technique to identify the problem it is critical that the leader explicitly challenges his/her team to support claims with evidence. *How do we know that is true? What evidence do we have?*

Sometimes the process of identifying the problem requires more research and data gathering. When this is the case it is essential to collect the data needed to adequately define the problem. The stakes are high and the extra time and patience pays off when all district efforts can begin with a thoughtful, evidence-based response to the question—*What problem are we trying to solve?*

Questions for Further Reflection

1. Reflect on a time you did not appropriately or sufficiently define the problem.
2. What were the consequences?
3. What strategies do you typically use to identify and define problems?
4. How do you ensure the time and human competencies needed on your work groups/teams/boards to effectively identify problems?

5. How do you know when you have identified the "right" problem?

Chapter Ten

Enacting Decisions and Leveraging Impact

> Once you make a decision, the universe conspires to make it happen. —Ralph Waldo Emerson

In previous chapters we reviewed different decision-making models and approaches to problem-solving. In each model, the most critical first step is accurately identifying and defining the problem. Choosing and adapting the right approach and implementing it with fidelity are also essential to effective decision-making practices. In other words, effective decision-making practices are not only about making the critical decisions, but also about *managing the consequences of decisions and creating and supporting the conditions to ensure the desired results.*

Some leaders are skilled and highly effective decision-makers regardless of the model they choose. There are other leaders, however, who consistently struggle with decision-making and as a result their decisions are difficult to enact and frequently fall short in terms of impact and effectiveness. This chapter will discuss what leaders can personally and organizationally do to improve their decision-making practices. It will also address how leaders can use decision-making as leverage for change.

BAD HABITS

In their *Harvard Business Review* post titled "9 Habits That Lead to Terrible Decisions,"[1] Jack Zenger and Joseph Folkman describe extensive research comparing leaders who were perceived to be good decision-makers to those who were not. They discovered *nine leader habits* that were most commonly associated with poor decision-making. Some of these behaviors were discussed previously as cognitive biases or traps. When these biases go unchecked and become routine for leaders they can become habitual practices that impact organizational effectiveness. The following paragraphs will describe these habits adapted to an educational leadership perspective.

The first bad habit is *laziness. This revealed itself as a failure to check facts, to take the initiative, to confirm assumptions, or to gather additional input*. These leaders were perceived to be sloppy in their work and unwilling to put themselves out. They often relied on past experience and expected results simply to be an extrapolation of the past.

Leaders can also develop the habit of *not anticipating unexpected events*. Generally speaking, the research supports the contention that if people just take the time to consider what might go wrong, they are actually very good at anticipating problems. Many leaders get so excited about a decision they are making that they never take the time to do that simple due diligence. This frequently happens when educational leaders attempt to add one new initiative (when staff are already feeling overwhelmed) without anticipating that something needs to be taken *off their plates*. The leader may also neglect to provide all the supports, like professional development, needed to make things work.

Indecisiveness is another habit that can impact organizational effectiveness. Complex decisions are difficult. When the data are continually changing and all the parts are in constant motion, it is common to become paralyzed with the desire for further analysis. This phenomenon, which we referred to previously as *analysis paralysis*, can be debilitating. When the analysis takes much longer than expected, poor decision-makers delay, opportunities are missed, and everyone is on hold. It takes courage for leaders to look at the data, consider the consequences responsibly, and then move forward. *Often indecision is worse than making the wrong decision.* How often do school leaders avoid making decisions or confronting difficult issues? When leaders are consistently indecisive or enable indecisiveness within their schools they are in essence relinquishing their responsibility as leaders, because *to lead is to decide.*

Some leaders are habitually *locked in the past*. They make poor decisions because they're using the same old data or processes they always have. Leaders can get comfortable with approaches that worked in the past and tend not to look for approaches that may work better. They are simply more comfortable with what they know. But, too often, when a decision is destined to go wrong, it's because the old process is based on assumptions that are no longer true. Poor decision-makers fail to reconsider those base assumptions when applying their tried and true practices.

Some leaders struggle with connecting and aligning their problem-solving to their overall strategies and greater goals. Their decision-making is *not strategically aligned.* In the absence of a clear strategy that provides context, many solutions may appear to make sense. When tightly linked to a clear strategy, however, the better, more high-impact solutions quickly begin to rise to the top. In an effort to better leverage decision-making to support organizational goals it is essential to ask the question, *how does this fit?*

Being *overly dependent* on others for decision-making is another bad habit. *Some decisions are never made because one person is waiting for another, who in turn is waiting for someone else's decision or input.* This is symptomatic of schools where people may feel powerless or fearful of making a mistake. It is also common in highly bureaucratic or departmentalized schools where no one makes a move because they don't want to "step on someone else's toes." As a result, nothing gets done. In a learning organization a leader must model, encourage, and make it psychologically safe for people to think independently and creatively to avoid inertia.

Leaders who work in *isolation* are also prone to poor decision-making. Involving others with the knowledge, experience, and expertise improves the quality of the decisions. Sometimes, however, people in leadership roles lack the necessary networking and relationship-building skills to access the right people and information. It is also possible that *lone wolf leaders* may choose not to involve others because they want the credit for a decision. Of course, this means they will also take the blame for the bad decisions.

Leaders cannot possibly be expected to know everything, but a *lack of technical depth* can make it difficult for the leader to comprehend what is important to know and what questions need to be asked. The problem is when decision-makers rely on others' knowledge and expertise without any perspective of their own, they have a difficult time integrating that information and evaluating it within a meaningful context.

District leaders are particularly susceptible to a lack of technical knowledge because they are required to make decisions in so many diverse arenas (legal, financial, public relations, political, curricular, instructional, and so on). It is important for educational leaders to know and understand their context and the implications of the decisions they face. It is also critical that leaders are skilled and resourceful in seeking out other talented people with expertise who can help them. This requires leaders to avoid the overconfidence bias trap by being comfortable and honest in acknowledging what they don't know.

Some leaders also *fail to communicate the what, where, when, and how associated with their decisions.* Good decisions can become bad decisions when people don't understand, or even know about them. Effective communication is essential to all aspects of leadership and particularly important when making and enacting a decision. Poor communication related to any aspect of the decision-making process can diminish the impact and ultimate success of the decision. For example, waiting too long for others' input, failing to recognize when something is relevant and needs to be considered, or failing to communicate the "why" or "how this impacts me," can contribute to an overall lack of engagement on the part of those expected to help implement the decision.

Each of these nine habits can readily be observed and practiced, either occasionally or frequently by school leaders. Sometimes, however, these habitual behaviors are deeply embedded within the culture of the school or district. When this is the case the leader not only needs to model "good habits" but she also needs to be explicit about embracing *a new way of doing business.* This often requires the leader to radically redesign the organizational architecture for decision-making. In other words, the leader must replace old "this is the way we have always done it" habits with thoughtful, proactive, evidence-based decision-making structures and practices.

These organizational practices at a very basic level include engaging others in deep levels of questioning, the thoughtful and proficient use of data, and the expectation for demonstrating evidence. In other words, are all members of the organization routinely asking the questions, *how do you know and what evidence do you have?*

A further consideration embedded in the culture is the degree of risk-taking or willingness to try new things and learn from mistakes. A school that has developed bad decision-making habits is also likely to be one where there is little personal and organizational learning and one where original thinking and innovation are stifled. It takes time and intentionality to transform these cultures—leaders need to begin by modeling trustworthy behaviors where a growth mindset individually and organizationally can flourish.

WHEN TO PERSIST

We discussed how the habits of leaders shape the architecture of decision-making in the organization and the quality of the decisions. We briefly examined factors influencing decision quality in chapter 7 and deepen our perspective here with the key assumption that ultimately the best (ethically sound) decision is *one that moves forward and is effectively supported and implemented.* In most complex situations there is not one *right* choice, but instead multiple potentially good options or paths forward. Choosing one option in a timely and appropriate fashion is essential, but as we know, the leader's responsibility does not end with choosing a course of action—the leader needs to engage in what it takes to set up the conditions to ensure that the decision is made "right."

Ensuring that the decision is "right" requires the leader to focus organizational efforts and deeply invest in what it takes to effectively enact the decision. Once the decision is made leaders need to strategically refocus attention to the routine daily actions that are required to make the choice succeed. This refocusing from the *work of making the decision* to *making the decision work* is critical. When this shift is made, the leader's personal and collective sense of efficacy is enhanced through focused and deliberate action.

At the same time it is important to acknowledge that although necessary, sometimes a deep level of investment in enacting decisions can become problematic. When leaders are deeply committed and personally invested in enacting a particular course of action it can become much more difficult to anticipate problems or measure progress objectively. Paradoxically, a strong investment in a particular course of action is both essential and a source of denial. The inability to see things objectively as we immerse ourselves in them is consistent with our natural tendencies toward biases, like confirmation and overconfidence.

The reality is that despite a leader's best intentions and efforts, sometimes decisions just don't work. Leaders need to routinely consider *how to balance one's commitment to a decision in order to make it the right decision, with the need to acknowledge and let go when it isn't working.* For educational leaders, always in the spotlight, this can be particularly challenging. One factor contributing to the challenge is that school governance is not structured for fluid thinking and adaptable processes. Board of Education meetings and protocols tend to be highly formalized and often politicized. There is typically little opportunity for creative thinking and deeper levels of discussion around practices. These public meetings have preset agendas that advance policies through voting and limit opportunities to reconsider options or creatively generate new ideas.

Leaders have a lot at stake in their decision-making. Working under highly visible conditions that are not conducive to learning from mistakes and quick and fluid adaptation—the question of accountability is typically complicated for educational leaders. Since leaders are always responsible for both the decision-making processes and outcomes, they need to consistently monitor and assess the impact of their decisions. Depending on the data collected through ongoing monitoring, the leader needs to explicitly choose *to continue with, or stop the implementation of a decision.* This is particularly challenging in schools where even though there is never a shortage of new initiatives (frequently too many initiatives), deep and meaningful change is slow and difficult to achieve.

In the *Harvard Business Review* blog post, "12 Guidelines for Deciding When to Persist, When to Quit,"[2] Rosabeth Moss Kanter shares several questions for leaders to consider when assessing whether to continue pursuing the hoped-for outcomes of a decision or give up on the pursuit. Of greatest significance to educational leaders are the following questions adapted from her work:

- Are the initial reasons for the efforts still valid? In what ways has the original context changed?
- Would the situation get worse if this effort stopped?
- Are leaders still enthusiastic, committed, and focused on the effort? What about other personnel? Students? Community members?
- Have sufficient resources been allocated or reallocated to adequately sustain the effort?
- Have critical deadlines and key milestones been met?
- Are there signs of progress, in that some problems have been solved, new activities are underway, and trends are positive?
- Is there a concrete achievement?

If leaders can answer *yes* (often in terms of degrees) to most of the questions, then there is good reason to persist.

This persistent action often requires ongoing decision-making. To fully embrace and persist the leader needs to thoughtfully choose to *let go* of some things along the way in order to equip the effort or initiative with the resources needed to flourish. With new efforts underway the leader needs to continually adapt and adjust as new information is learned and the context changes. In other words, educational leaders need to constantly scaffold the work to make a "good option" the right one.

ETHICALLY AND SOCIALLY JUST DECISION-MAKING

Underlying all decision-making efforts are deeply held values that uphold ethical, socially just, and equitable practices. One's personal and professional code of ethics and standards are lenses that provide an essential multifaceted perspective when enacting and evaluating the appropriateness and effectiveness of our decisions. Daniel Pink offers a quick self-check when considering whether a decision is appropriate.[3] He suggests that you "think about the story the graceful, wise, awesome 90-year-old version of you will want to tell. And just don't do something that person will regret."

In all aspects of making and implementing decisions it is critical to consider—*who benefits from the decision and how?* Answers to these questions in schools are most clearly evidenced in the allocation of resources. When enacting a decision do the resource allocation implications benefit some students more than others? For example, if your staffing allocation is based on a simple formula that applies equally to all schools, but the student needs at some schools are significantly greater, the process is inherently not equitable. Treating everyone equally is not the same as treating everyone equitably.

LEVERAGING IMPACT

Throughout the book we have discussed decision-making and problem-solving from a wide array of perspectives. Leadership is about making decisions and solving problems. When leaders think and act strategically there is a sense of coherence, alignment, and forward motion in these efforts.

In all circumstances, decisions and problems can provide excellent leverage for change. Sometimes the problem presents itself, other times the leader needs to find the *right* problem in order to impact change and continually improve. In other words, leaders don't just react or respond to existing problems. They actively seek problems through persistent questioning, data collection, and by scanning the larger environment for patterns and changing trends. Leaders can use their social networks and a wide array of analytical tools to help them understand what factors will likely impact their organizations and communities.

Problems can be found everywhere so leaders need to be thoughtful about finding and focusing on the *right* problems. The *right* problems focus on serving the greater good through socially just practices and advance collective efforts to pursue a shared vision of excellence for all.

Questions for Further Reflection

1. Consider each of the bad habits discussed. What habits are the most problematic for you? For your school or district?
2. Consider a recent decision you made—how did you make it the "right" decision?
3. Was there a time you persisted with a decision when you should have let it go?
4. How do you ensure that you enact your decisions in an ethical and socially just way?
5. How do you *find* problems?

Conclusion

When we *decide to lead* we courageously commit to being decision-makers. We strive to understand, think about, and design the conditions for effective decision-making because we understand that through our decision-making we can leverage organizational change for the greater good. We can make a difference!

We grow to appreciate that this core leadership work is enhanced (both personally and for our organizations) by what we *know, think, and do*. Specifically, what we *know* about self, others, and our context; how we *think and understand* systems, cognitive forces, and conceptual frames; *and what we do*—build capacity in others, design the architecture for decision-making, and employ different processes.

As decision-makers we learn that our ability to be effective in a rapidly changing, complex environment requires us to constantly learn and adapt. We need to recognize what we don't know, think in deeper more sophisticated ways, and build our capacity through the constant flow of ideas and interactions with others. We recognize our many limitations while at the same time consistently strive to become better at navigating imperfect conditions in an irrational world.

Most importantly, we are deeply grateful for the responsibility to decide. As leaders we see *possibilities in every decision and opportunities in every problem.*

Resources

The following templates can be used for logging and tracking decisions and assessing decision quality. These tools can be used individually or collectively with team members to help reflect on the nature, process, and effectiveness of organizational decision-making.

- Decision-Making Profile 1
- Decision-Making Profile 2
- Decision Quality Assessment

DECISION-MAKING PROFILE 1

Log the decisions you make over the course of a week. (Consider decisions related to personnel, staffing, students, parents, community, BOE, curriculum, instruction, budget, safety, etc.)

Please record the general topic and the decision that was made.

Decision Area	Nature of Decision
(example: Staffing)	(Reduced FTE allocation in Fine Arts)
1.	
2.	
3.	
4.	
5.	
6.	
7.	
8.	
9.	
10.	

DECISION-MAKING PROFILE 2

Using the ten decisions logged on template 1, respond to the following:

Decision	React or Initiate	Intuitive, Blended (intuitive & heuristic) or Formal Analysis	Were there heuristics/short-cuts used? What were they?	Who was involved in process?
1.				
2.				
3.				
4.				
5.				
6.				
7.				
8.				
9.				
10.				

DECISION QUALITY ASSESSMENT

In assessing the *quality of a decision*,[1] it may be helpful to consider the presence of the following:

- A clear understanding of the problem.
- A number of creative, manageable alternatives from which to choose.
- Meaningful information/data that are reliable and unbiased (to the extent possible).
- Clarity about desired outcomes (consistent with short- and long-term goals/vision).
- Ownership/commitment to act by all stakeholders necessary to achieve effective action.

Quality

When looking back at the decisions recorded, I believe it was the right course of action:

4 = most of the time
3 = some of the time
2 = infrequently
1 = never

Evidence/Indicators/Comments:

Efficiency: Speed

The time it took to make the decisions was:

4 = reasonable/balanced given my time and the potential impact of the decision
3 = a bit too fast given the potential impact/consequences
2 = a bit too slow given the potential impact/consequences
1= much too fast or slow

Evidence/Indicators/Comments:

Efficiency: Effort

In making and executing the decisions I/we put in:

4 = exactly the right amount of effort
3 = somewhat too much effort
2 = somewhat too little effort
1 = way too much/nowhere near enough effort

Evidence/Indicators/Comments:

Participation/Process

Level of engagement/delegation in the decision process was:

4 = appropriate
3 = a little too high
2 = a little too low
1 = way too high/low

Evidence/Indicators/Comments:

Execution

The decisions resulted in the intended action/direction:

4 = most of the time
3 = some of the time
2 = infrequently
1= never

Evidence/Indicators/Comments:

Other contextual considerations**:**

1. *Is there a clear understanding of our context? Where we are, where we are going, and what we are trying to accomplish?* What do the data tell us about our current reality? How does the decision we are assessing align with our values and mission and further advance our vision?
2. *Are we using the right drivers*? To what extent do the drivers (employed in the process and decision) have high impact?
3. *Have we considered our situation from a variety of organizational frames?* To what extent have we "reframed" to consider the situation from a variety of perspectives?

4. *What is the level of complexity?* Was the problem and ultimate decision appropriately identified?
5. *What is our personal understanding of the degree of change needed?* Does the decision process and outcome support the level of change we believe is necessary?
6. *How do we perceive our role and the roles of others in leading change and ensuring equity and social justice?* To what extent does the process and outcome reflect leaders acting as *agents of change* or *managers of the status quo*? To what extent did others have a voice in the decision-making process?
7. *Do the decisions meet our ethical standards?* The following questions adapted from the *Josephson Institute of Ethics* can serve as a guide for personal reflection in assessing the ethical quality of the decision.

   - Does the decision conflict with any core ethical values?
   - How does the decision affect others?
   - Are the actions legal?
   - How would the decision look if it were reported on the news or in another public forum?
   - How would reasonable people perceive the decision?
   - Can you rationally and honestly defend the decision?

Notes

1. IN SEARCH OF SELF

1. Daniel Goleman, "What Makes a Leader," *Harvard Business Review* 76 (November/December 1998): 93–102.
2. Dan Ariely, *Predictably Irrational: The Hidden Forces That Shape Our Decisions* (New York: HarperCollins, 2008).
3. R. Fisher and Dan Shapiro, *Beyond Reason: Using Emotions as You Negotiate* (New York: Penguin, 2005).
4. The Leadership Circle, "The Leadership Circle Overview with Bob Anderson," YouTube. 2011. Accessed June 1, 2016, at https://www.youtube.com/watch?v=dU--dtTZOA0.
5. Herminia Ibarra, "The Authenticity Paradox," *Harvard Business Review* 93, no. 1/2 (Jan/Feb. 2015): 54–59.
6. Ibarra, "The Authenticity Paradox," 56.
7. Carol S. Dweck, *Mindset: The New Psychology of Success* (New York: Ballantine Books, 2006), 6.
8. www.ted.com/talks/julia_galef_why_you_think_you_re_right_even_if_you_re_wrong?utm_source=newsletter_weekly_2016-07-02&utm_campaign=newsletter_w.
9. Maya Angelou, Accessed June 10, 2016, http://www.brainyquote.com/quotes/authors/m/maya_angelou.html
10. Stephen Uebbing and Mike Ford, *The Life Cycle of Leadership: Surviving and Thriving in Today's Schools* (Oxford, OH: Learning Forward, 2010).
11. Uebbing and Ford, *The Life Cycle of Leadership.*
12. David Brooks, *Road to Character* (New York: Random House, 2015).

2. MOTIVATION, TRUST, AND ENGAGEMENT

1. Reference for Business, "Theory X and Theory Y." Accessed May 15, 2016. www.referenceforbusiness.com/management/Str-Ti/Theory-X-and-Theory-Y.html#ixzz3Vc9Q0o1b.
2. Daniel Pink, *Drive: The Surprising Truth about What Motivates Us* (New York: Riverhead Books, 2009).
3. Sydney Finkelstein, "Secrets of Superbosses," *Harvard Business Review* 94, no. 1 (Jan/Feb 2016): 104–7.

4. Sharon D. Kruse and Karen Seashore Louis, *Building Strong School Cultures* (Thousand Oaks, CA: Corwin Press, 2009).
5. Colin Powell press conference: www.youtube.com/watch?v=ocSw1m30UBI.
6. Julie P. Combs, Stacey Edmonson, and Sandra Harris, *The Trust Factor: Strategies for School Leaders* (Larchmont, NY: Eye on Education, 2013).
7. Sarah Barto, "An Introduction to Employee Engagement," AON Hewitt Consulting, presented January 24, 2015, University of Illinois School Executive Leadership Program.
8. Barto, "An Introduction to Employee Engagement."

3. COMMUNITY AND CONTEXT

1. John Donahue and Mark Moore, eds., *Ports in a Storm: Public Management in a Turbulent World* (Washington, DC: Brookings Institution Press, 2012).
2. Willona M. Sloan, "What Is the Purpose of Education," *Education Update* 54, no.7 (July 2012). http://www.ascd.org/publications/newsletters/education-update/jul12/vol54/num07/What-Is-the-Purpose-of-Education¢.aspx.
3. Thomas Armstrong, *The Best Schools: How Human Development Research Should Inform Educational Practice* (Alexandria, VA: ASCD, 2006), 34–67.

4. FORCES THAT SHAPE OUR DECISIONS

1. Daniel Kahneman, *Thinking Fast and Slow* (New York: Farrar, Straus and Giroux, 2011), 21–24.
2. Daniel Kahneman, 2011, https://www.youtube.com/watch?v=CjVQJdIrDJ0.
3. MindTools, Avoiding Psychological Bias in Decision-Making, https://www.mindtools.com/pages/article/avoiding-psychological-bias.htm.
4. Francesca Gino, "How Anxiety Can Lead Your Decisions Astray," *Harvard Business Review*, 2013. Accessed June 15, 2016, https://hbr.org/2013/10/how-anxiety-can-lead-your-decisions-astray/.
5. Emre Soyer and Robin M. Hogarth, "Fooled by Experience," *Harvard Business Review* 98, no. 5 (May 2015): 72–77.
6. Howard Ross, "3 Ways to Make Less Biased Decisions." *Harvard Business Review*, 2015. Accessed June 16, 2016, https://hbr.org/2015/04/3-ways-to-make-less-biased-decisions.
7. James Lytle and Harris Sokoloff, "A Complex Web: The New Normal for Superintendents," *School Administrator* 7, no. 8 (September 2013): 20–25.

5. FRAMES THAT GUIDE DECISION-MAKING

1. Justin Fox, "From Economic Man to Behavioral Economics," *Harvard Business Review* 93, no. 5 (May 2015): 78–85.
2. Lee Bolman and Terrence Deal, *Reframing Organizations: Artistry, Choice and Leadership*, 4th ed. (San Francisco: Jossey-Bass, 2008).
3. Bolman and Deal, *Reframing Organizations*, 18.
4. David J. Snowden and Mary E. Boone, "A Leader's Framework for Decision-Making," *Harvard Business Review* 85, no. 11 (Nov. 2007): 68–76.

6. BUILDING CAPACITY

1. N. Christakis and J. Fowler, *Connected: The Surprising Power of Our Social Networks and How They Shape Our Lives* (New York: Little, Brown and Company, 2011).
2. Michael Fullan, *Choosing the Wrong Drivers for Whole System Reform*, Centre for Strategic Education, Seminar Series Paper No. 204, May 2011.
3. Jon R. Katzenbach and Douglas K. Smith, "The Discipline of Teams," *Harvard Business Review* 83, no. 7/8 (July/August 2005): 162–71.
4. Susan A. Wheelan, *Creating Effective Teams*, 5th ed. (Thousand Oaks, CA: Sage, 2014).
5. Wheelan, *Creating Effective Teams*, 7–10.
6. Wayne Hoy and John Tarter, *Administrators Solving the Problems of Practice* (Boston: Pearson Education, 2008), 10–13.
7. Kathryn Boudett and Elizabeth City, *Meeting Wise: Making the Most of Collaborative Time for Educators* (Cambridge, MA: Harvard Education Press, 2014).
8. Boudett and City, *Meeting Wise*, 11.

7. BUILDING THE ARCHITECTURE FOR DECISION-MAKING

1. Richard Thaler and Cass R. Sunstein, *Nudge: Improving Decisions about Wealth, Health and Happiness* (New York: Penguin, 2009).
2. Larry Neal and Carl Spetzler, "An Organization-Wide Approach to Good Decision Making," *Harvard Business Review*, 2015. Accessed June 16, 2016, https://hbr.org/2015/05/an-organization-wide-approach-to-good-decision-making.
3. Thomas Davenport, "The Big Lesson from 12 Good Decisions," *Harvard Business Review*, October 28, 2013.
4. Davenport, "The Big Lesson from 12 Good Decisions."
5. Neal and Spetzler, "An Organization-Wide Approach to Good Decision-Making."
6. Michael Fullan, "Choosing the Wrong Drivers for Whole System Reform," Centre for Strategic Education, Seminar Series Paper No. 204, May 2011.
7. Lee Bolman and Terrence Deal, *Reframing Organizations: Artistry, Choice and Leadership*, 4th ed. (San Francisco: Jossey-Bass, 2008).
8. Josephson Institute of Ethics. Accessed May 12, 2016. http://josephsoninstitute.org.
9. Alex Pentland, "Beyond the Echo Chamber," *Harvard Business Review* 91, no 11 (November 2013): 80–86.
10. Pentland, "Beyond the Echo Chamber," 83.

8. DECIDING HOW TO DECIDE

1. Wayne Hoy and John Tarter, *Administrators Solving the Problems of Practice* (Boston: Pearson Education, 2008), 10–13.
2. Hoy and Tarter, *Administrators Solving the Problems of Practice*, 12.
3. Hoy and Tarter, *Administrators Solving the Problems of Practice*, 13.
4. Josephson Institute of Ethics. Accessed May 12, 2016. http://josephsoninstitute.org.
5. "Decision-Making Techniques: How to Make Better Decisions." Decision-Making Techniques and Skills from MindTools.com. Accessed June 15, 2016.
6. Min Basadur, "The Simplex Model." Applied Creativity. Accessed June 14, 2016. http://www.basadur.com/howwedoit/an8stepprocess/tabid/82/default.aspx.
7. "The Recognition Primed Decision (RPD) Process." Mind Tools Corporate.

8. "OODA Loops: Understanding the Decision Cycle." OODA Loops. Accessed June 16, 2016. https://www.mindtools.com/pages/article/newTED_78.htm.

9. DEFINING THE PROBLEM

1. "Decision-Making Techniques: How to Make Better Decisions." Decision-Making Techniques and Skills from MindTools.com. Accessed June 15, 2016. https://www.mindtools.com/pages/main/newMN_TED.htm.

2. "CATWOE: Developing a Robust Problem Definition." CATWOE. Accessed June 16, 2016. https://www.mindtools.com/pages/article/newTMC_83.htm.

3. "Root Cause Analysis: Tracing a Problem to Its Origins." Root Cause Analysis. Accessed June 17, 2016. https://www.mindtools.com/pages/article/newTMC_80.htm.

10. ENACTING DECISIONS AND LEVERAGING IMPACT

1. Jack Zenger and Joseph Folkman, "9 Habits That Lead to Terrible Decisions," *Harvard Business Review*, 2014. Accessed March 10, 2016, https://hbr.org/2014/09/9-habits-that-lead-to-terrible-decisions/.

2. Rosabeth Moss Kanter, "12 Guidelines for Deciding When to Persist, When to Quit," *Harvard Business Review*, 2012. Accessed June 16, 2016, https://hbr.org/2012/10/12-guidelines-for-deciding-whe/.

3. http://www.danpink.com.

RESOURCES

1. Adapted from L. Neal and C. Spetzler, "An Organization-Wide Approach to Good Decision Making," *Harvard Business Review*, 2015. Accessed June 16, 2016, https://hbr.org/2015/05/an-organization-wide-approach-to-good-decision-making.

References

Ariely, Daniel. *Predictably Irrational: The Hidden Forces That Shape Our Decisions*. New York: HarperCollins, 2008.

Armstrong, Thomas. *The Best Schools: How Human Development Research Should Inform Educational Practice*. Alexandria, VA: ASCD, 2006.

Basadur, Min. "The Simplex Model." Applied Creativity. Accessed June 14, 2016. http://www.basadur.com/howwedoit/an8stepprocess/tabid/82/default.aspx.

Beshears, John, and Francesca Gino. "Leaders as Decision Architects." *Harvard Business Review* 93, no. 5 (May 2015): 51–62.

Bolman, Lee, and Terrence Deal. *Reframing Organizations: Artistry, Choice and Leadership*, 4th ed. San Francisco: Jossey-Bass, 2008.

Boudett, Kathryn, and Elizabeth City. *Meeting Wise: Making the Most of Collaborative Time for Educators*. Cambridge, MA: Harvard Education Press, 2014.

Brooks, David. *Road to Character*. New York: Random House, 2015.

"CATWOE: Developing a Robust Problem Definition." CATWOE. Accessed June 16, 2016. https://www.mindtools.com/pages/article/newTMC_83.htm.

Christakis, N., and J. Fowler. *Connected: The Surprising Power of Our Social Networks and How They Shape Our Lives*. New York: Little, Brown and Company, 2011.

Combs, Julie P., Stacey Edmonson, and Sandra Harris. *The Trust Factor: Strategies for School Leaders*. Larchmont, NY: Eye on Education, 2013.

"The Cynefin Framework: Using the Most Appropriate Problem-Solving Process." The Cynefin Framework. Accessed June 15, 2016, https://www.mindtools.com/pages/article/cynefin-framework.htm.

Davenport, Thomas. "The Big Lesson from 12 Good Decisions." *Harvard Business Review*, October 28, 2013.

"Decision-Making Techniques: How to Make Better Decisions." Decision-Making Techniques and Skills from MindTools.com. Accessed June 15, 2016. https://www.mindtools.com/pages/main/newMN_TED.htm.

Donahue, John, and Mark Moore, eds. *Ports in a Storm: Public Management in a Turbulent World*. Washington, DC: Brookings Institution Press, 2012.

Dweck, Carol S. *Mindset: The New Psychology of Success*. New York: Ballantine Books, 2006.

Finkelstein, Sydney. "Secrets of Superbosses." *Harvard Business Review* 94, no. 1 (January/February 2016): 104–7.

Fisher, R., and Dan Shapiro. *Beyond Reason: Using Emotions as You Negotiate*. New York: Penguin Group, 2005.

Fox, Justin. "From Economic Man to Behavioral Economics." *Harvard Business Review* 93, no. 5 (May 2015): 78–85.

Fullan, Michael. "Choosing the Wrong Drivers for Whole System Reform." Seminar Series Paper No.10, Centre for Strategic Education, May 2011.

Gino, Francesca. "How Anxiety Can Lead Your Decisions Astray." *Harvard Business Review*, 2013. Accessed June 15, 2016. https://hbr.org/2013/10/how-anxiety-can-lead-your-decisions-astray/.

Goleman, Daniel. "What Makes a Leader." *Harvard Business Review* 76, no. 6 (November/December 1998): 93–102.

Hoy, Wayne, and John Tarter. *Administrators Solving the Problems of Practice*, 3rd ed. Boston: Pearson Education, 2008.

Ibarra, Herminia. "The Authenticity Paradox." *Harvard Business Review* 93, no. 1/2 (January/February 2015): 54–59.

Josephson Institute of Ethics. Accessed May 12, 2016, http://josephsoninstitute.org

Kahneman, Daniel. *Thinking Fast and Slow*. New York: Farrar, Straus and Giroux, 2011.

Katzenbach, Jon R., and Douglas K. Smith. "The Discipline of Teams." *Harvard Business Review* 83, no. 7/8 (July/August 2005): 162–71.

Kegan, Robert, and Lisa Laskow Lahey. *Immunity to Change.* Boston: Harvard Business Press, 2009.

Kruse, Sharon D., and Karen Seashore Louis. *Building Strong School Cultures.* Thousand Oaks, CA: Corwin Press, 2009.

The Leadership Circle. "The Leadership Circle Overview with Bob Anderson." YouTube. 2011. Accessed June 1, 2016, at https://www.youtube.com/watch?v=dU--dtTZOA0.

Lytle, James, and Harris Sokoloff. "A Complex Web: The New Normal for Superintendents." *School Administrator* 7, no. 8 (September 2013): 20–25.

Moss Kanter, Rosabeth, "12 Guidelines for Deciding When to Persist, When to Quit." *Harvard Business Review*. 2012. Accessed June 16, 2016. https://hbr.org/2012/10/12-guidelines-for-deciding-whe/.

Neal, L., and C. Spetzler. "An Organization-Wide Approach to Good Decision Making." *Harvard Business Review*, 2015. Accessed June 16, 2016, https://hbr.org/2015/05/an-organization-wide-approach-to-good-decision-making.

"OODA Loops: Understanding the Decision Cycle." OODA Loops. Accessed June 16, 2016, https://www.mindtools.com/pages/article/newTED_78.htm.

Pentland, Alex. "Beyond the Echo Chamber." *Harvard Business Review* 91, no 11 (November 2013): 80–86.

Pink, Daniel. *Drive: The Surprising Truth about What Motivates Us.* New York: Riverhead Books, 2009.

Reference for Business. "Theory X and Theory Y." Accessed May 15, 2016, http://www.referenceforbusiness.com/management/Str-Ti/Theory-X-and-Theory-Y.html#ixzz3Vc9Q0o1b.

"Root Cause Analysis: Tracing a Problem to Its Origins." Root Cause Analysis. Accessed June 17, 2016, https://www.mindtools.com/pages/article/newTMC_80.htm.

Rose, Mike. *Why School? Reclaiming Education for All of Us.* New York: New Press, 2009.

Ross, Howard. "3 Ways to Make Less Biased Decisions." *Harvard Business Review*. 2015. Accessed June 16, 2016, https://hbr.org/2015/04/3-ways-to-make-less-biased-decisions.

Sloan, Willona M. "What Is the Purpose of Education." *Education Update* 54, no. 7 (July 2012). http://www.ascd.org/publications/newsletters/education-update/jul12/vol54/num07/What-Is-the-Purpose-of-Education¢.aspx.

Snowden, David J., and Mary E. Boone. "A Leader's Framework for Decision-Making." *Harvard Business Review* 85, no. 11 (November 2007): 68–76.

Soyer, Emre, and Robin M. Hogarth. "Fooled by Experience." *Harvard Business Review* 98, no. 5 (May 2015): 72–77.

Spradlin, Dwayne. "Are You Solving the Right Problem?" *Harvard Business Review* 90, no. 9 (September 2012): 84–93.

Thaler, Richard, and Cass R. Sunstein. *Nudge: Improving Decisions about Wealth, Health and Happiness.* New York: Penguin, 2009.

Uebbing, Stephen, and Mike Ford. *The Life Cycle of Leadership: Surviving and Thriving in Today's Schools*. Oxford, OH: Learning Forward, 2010.

Wheelan, Susan A. *Creating Effective Teams*, 5th ed. Thousand Oaks, CA: Sage, 2014.

Zenger, Jack, and Joseph Folkman. "9 Habits That Lead to Terrible Decisions." *Harvard Business Review*, 2014. Accessed March 10, 2016, https://hbr.org/2014/09/9-habits-that-lead-to-terrible-decisions/.

About the Author

Mary B. Herrmann is a clinical assistant professor in the Education Policy, Organization and Leadership Department at the University of Illinois at Urbana-Champaign. Her primary scholarship interests include leadership development, decision-making, organizational learning, and improvement. Herrmann is particularly focused on the social, psychological, and ethical dimensions of leadership in her clinical work with aspiring principals and superintendents. She has written several articles for the *School Administrator* and serves as a book reviewer for the American Association of School Administrators.

Herrmann has extensive PK–12 leadership experience. She has served as an assistant principal, principal, assistant superintendent, and superintendent in multiple high performing school districts throughout the Midwest. She has had appointments on several professional boards and foundations and is currently serving in an elected official role as a Village trustee.